Never A Dull Moment

Teresa Holmgren

DEDICATION

To my mother and father,
Mable Hall Seibert
and
H. Van Seibert,
who were my first and best teachers.

To Randee and Dorothy, my first classroom team.
You both left this earth too soon, but I feel your influence
in my classroom every day.

ACKNOWLEDGMENTS

Loving thanks to my husband, Ronald, who has always urged me to be who I need to be. He has patiently encouraged me to write when I must, supporting me in all those inconvenient moments when my writing has seized me, and he has pushed me forward when I doubted for even a moment.

Also, special gratitude to my sisters, Sharon and Marilyn, who are also teachers. They have been great examples and have always watched out for their little sis.

I am also extremely grateful to the magnificent teachers, associates, social workers, counselors, and administrators with whom I have taught. As my peers, my friends, and my confidants, they have all greatly enriched my life.

The greatest contributors to this book, however, have been the students in my first classroom. The life lessons they taught me were spectacular and life-changing. God bless them all.

1   THERE ARE WORSE THINGS THAN BEING HUNGRY

Mark was a student in my "higher functioning" classroom of intellectually challenged teenagers. Back then, in the early 1970s, these kids were labelled as EMR, Educable Mentally Retarded. In short, Mark looked normal, but he was smart enough to know he wasn't normal.

Mark's mother was a prostitute. They lived in the high-rise "projects" on the north side of the large metropolitan city where I taught. He was a little short for seventeen (about 5'4"), very slender, and looked even more slender in his too-small jeans and plaid shirts. He had shoulder-length brown hair with bangs. (It WAS the 1970s) He had a pleasant face with round brown eyes, but rarely smiled. Life was rough for him.

He had been traumatized, I figured, by living in a situation where his mother would answer their door, let a man in, tell Mark to stay in the living room with the TV blaring, and take her "john" back to the bedroom. One time, early in the fall, Mark missed a whole week of school. The school social worker told me that Mark had been staying in a temporary foster home for the week and was getting some counseling. When Mark returned to class, he calmly relayed the story of what had happened; apparently, he witnessed the suicide of his mother's pimp. The man simply jumped out of the window in Mark's fifth floor apartment. But now, Mom was back in business and Mark was back at home.

This created another problem. That now-deceased pimp had been Mark's transportation to and from school. There should have been a school bus, but his mother had been very unreliable at getting Mark up and ready for school in time to keep the bus on schedule, so she agreed to get him there without the help of the school system. Now, he had no ride to school. The social worker was a short-term solution. I needed to teach Mark to ride the city bus. He would need to know how to ride it when he graduated and got a job, so now was a good time to learn.

Well, I grew up on a farm. I had never really spent much time even walking on a city sidewalk, let alone riding a city bus. Mark and I learned together. He caught on quickly, even doing a great job asking the driver for a transfer, but he had one looming fear. People in his project neighborhood were regularly mugged. His mother wasn't worried. She was confident that "the folks who live here won't mess with my boy. They know better." She forgot her enforcer was dead, and sure enough, Mark was robbed of his watch and wallet the first time he rode home alone from school. It was just after Thanksgiving, and Mark's holiday season was about to get worse.

There was a horrible flu going around. Mark became ill two weeks before Christmas vacation started. Joyce, the social worker, checked on him a couple times a week. She reported to me that although he was over the worst of it, he was still weak and recovering slowly.

Mark would miss the big Santa Party we had every year. Our special education school had about 200 students attending. Right before vacation, a wonderful Santa would enter the gym, where we had gathered all the children. It was chaos. Santa would read each name from a list. The students would take their turns walking up on the stage (or be taken up there in their wheelchair) where Santa was seated on his throne. Santa would bestow each child with a large bag of wrapped gifts for them to take home and open. The social worker planned to take Mark's gifts to his apartment, so I briefly quit worrying.

I started worrying again, right after lunch that day, when Mark showed up for school. He could barely walk. We had already finished gathering all the kids around the edge of the gym. They were being led in a raucous chorus of holiday songs, so I seated Mark on one of the staff chairs and waited with him for the singing to end and the present distribution to begin. When Santa called his name, Mark struggled to his feet, nearly knocking over the folding chair where he was sitting. I stood up to reach for him, but he fainted, falling at my feet. Miss Pauline, who was the school nurse, along with Joyce and the principal, helped me carry him to the nurse's office. We placed him gently on her padded wooden cot and applied damp cloths to his clammy forehead.

He awakened after a short time, and had no idea where he was. When he saw the four of us there together, he said, "I came to school."

Mark was lying on that cot, looking so very pale and incredibly frail. He truly looked like he should have been in the hospital. We phoned his mother, who had no idea he was not in his room at home. We discussed taking him to the hospital across the street, but Pauline concluded that he was not dehydrated or in need of emergency care, so Joyce and I agreed to give him a ride home. I went down to the gym to get Mark's bag of presents and put them in my car. When I returned to the nurse's office to get Mark, he was asleep. We let him rest for about an hour.

When Mark woke up, I gave him some graham crackers and juice. He sat on the edge of the cot, eating slowly, and we spent a few minutes talking about what had been going on at school while he had been out sick. He mostly listened and ate, and then he apologized for being "so much trouble." I assured him that we did not consider him any trouble and that we were the ones who felt badly. I explained that we had hoped he would regain his strength over the two weeks of Christmas Break.

Then I asked the question. To this day, I have not forgotten this. It was innocent enough and really, a natural question to ask. I was expressing concern over the possibility that he could have collapsed on the city bus or on the street....that he could have been injured.

"Mark, why did you try to come to school when you were so weak?"

He replied, "I knew this was the only Christmas I would have,"

Yeah, let that sink in for a minute. I didn't have a minute. It hit all of us in the room like a brick; the social worker, the nurse, and I. We all moved straight to Mark and embraced him. He was so physically delicate at this point; let me assure you it was a light embrace; much lighter than we would have preferred to have given him.

Mark said, through his tears, "I love you."

We replied that we loved him, and the four of us just stood there, together, for a bit longer. Feeling that love.

Pauline got him bundled up in his coat, adding a warm scarf, hat, and mittens from her closet. Joyce went to her office pantry to get some extra food for Mark to take home. I went to warm up my car.

It was a quick ride to the bitterly cold near-north side of the downtown area. I told Mark to stay in his apartment over the winter break and to rest up. Then, I waited in the car while Joyce helped Mark get inside, and while she took in the presents and the food.

That was the last time I saw Mark. When Joyce tried to contact them during break, she discovered they had left the day after we dropped him off. The neighbor said they "went to Chicago for Christmas." Despite several attempts, Joyce could never locate them after that.

Mark, wherever you are, I hope that awful Christmas has faded from your memory. The only part I don't want you to forget is that you are loved. Love can get you through being ill, being lonely, being neglected, even being hungry. I hope that wherever you are now, you are wanted, fed, cared for, and loved by those around you.

Mark, wherever you are now, I want to thank you for this lesson in life. It's not the presents, the food, or the festivities that make Christmas or any occasion important. It's love....simply the human love we have for each other. Without love, as the famous book says, we are nothing.

2 BEFORE AUTISM WAS AN EPIDEMIC

Corey had beautiful eyes....well, I thought they were beautiful. They were the most charming, warm, brown eyes I had ever seen in a child. You had to look him in the eyes; they just drew you in. But Corey could not maintain eye contact for any length of time. He was a savant; an artistic savant; a savant with autism.

He echoed what you said, but was unable to construct an answer for any question he was asked, like "What did Corey have for breakfast?" He would just smile and reply, "Corey have for breakfast?"

He rocked. His arms would flail in mid-air at times of excitement or confusion. When he stood still and was not asked any questions, he appeared to be pretty normal; a handsome, tall, well-built, African-American sixteen year old. His single mother was a hotel maid. Corey adored her. He very seldom was unhappy. He smiled when spoken to and tried dutifully to follow directions. His mother had raised him to be a gentleman; he opened doors for me and would try to relieve me of any large loads he might see me carrying. I still wish I could have relieved Corey of his burden; and freed him to fully express his monumental talent. Autism doesn't work like that.

I know this now, because I have a grandson with autism. He is also a savant, being hyperlexic, an expert on exotic animals, and also a calendar savant. His art, sense of humor, and creativity are impressive.

However, Corey was my first contact with autism, back in 1974. Educators certainly did not know everything we now know about it. There was very little information. There was no mention of autism in my college classes.

Corey was in my classroom of mentally challenged, mentally ill, higher-functioning high school students. He fit right in. Except for that art thing.

Back then, copies were made on mimeograph machines. Purple ink, damp stinky paper... the kind of smell we used to pretend to get "high" on. Pretty toxic stuff. There were no Xerox machines or copy machines as we know them today. There was certainly no way to enlarge or reduce pictures; unless you had Corey in your room. Corey could draw them exactly like they were printed, any size I needed. He had multiple fancy fonts, also. Flawlessly executed.

How to channel that talent? Or was it OK to just let him use it for his own amusement? He had no friends, so Corey had never been invited to a sleepover, or a birthday party, or gone on a date. He wasn't going to get his driver's license or go to a football game or the prom. His entire source of 'fun' was his drawing. Maybe we should just leave the kid alone and let him draw. Don't try to turn him into 'something'.

I was a young, enthusiastic teacher. I had to try.....try

something. I entered him in the nearby state university "World Law Day" poster competition. He would be competing with twenty extremely talented high school artists from all over the state. I sat him down with a box of markers, showed him the promotional materials from the event, and he began drawing. His first drawing was a beautiful rendition of the globe, with tall white columns all around it, and a collection of multi-cultural faces. He added some of his magazine-ready script, and he had the winning entry done in about twenty minutes.

Corey was not really public appearance material, so his mother would not allow him to go accept his award. Disappointed, but understanding, I accepted a shiny plaque and the $100.00 prize for him.

His mother and I, with our school's art teacher, brainstormed ways to spend the money on Corey. Art books? A day at the local amusement mega-park? New clothes? Markers and art paper?

We chose an exquisite calligraphy set. Corey's mother felt he might be able to help them earn some extra money if he could create handmade monogrammed card sets. He loved to make ornate script letters, but they would be more marketable if they were not done with markers. She bought some high-quality plain cards from a stationery supplier and intended to have him make sets of cards. She would market them in packages of six or eight cards in boutiques around the city. It seemed like a good plan; entrepreneurial, but simple. All the staff at the school bought some. They were really beautiful, but there was a serious problem. Corey started to balk at making them. He was, of course, unable to explain himself, but he made it quite clear; "No." "All done." These were bold self-assertions for an echolalic; his own brief opinions about this repetitive and uninspired task. He had done some to humor us, but this was not the way he wanted to express his art.

In what seemed to be a dramatic protest, Corey drastically changed his style of drawing. He drew fewer small pictures and almost no script. He began drawing poster-sized illustrations of wild animals, which were subjects he had never done before. When my classroom moved to the basement of one of the high schools, the principal there insisted on purchasing a drawing of a cougar that Corey had done. He had it professionally framed, and placed it on the wall behind his desk. It looked like it had come from an expensive wildlife gallery. After we encouraged Corey to do a few more similar drawings of other wild animals, he caught on, and switched to pictures of farm animals and Native Americans.

His mother realized what was going on with his efforts to undermine our joint efforts to commercialize his creativity, and she wisely put a stop to it all. She knew Corey better than anyone else. She realized that despite her (and our) well-intentioned efforts to help her only son find a way that would allow him to generate an income as an adult, Corey wanted no part of it. He just wanted to draw. He wanted to draw what he wanted, when he wanted, and he wanted everyone to stop taking it away from him and selling it.

Lesson learned.

Oh, did I mention the name of the school where I taught? The name of the school where Corey taught me this lesson? The name was Emerson School.

This school was named after Ralph Waldo Emerson,

that feisty mid-19th century champion of individualism and being true to your "nature". That's all Corey really wanted to do. His caretaker and teachers wanted to make him into something special. He already was something special; he was Corey.

No one said it better than Ralph Waldo Emerson himself, "It is easy to live for others, everyone does. I call on you to live for yourself."

Over all the years I have been a teacher, and as a mother of five children, this lesson has perhaps been one of the most valuable. Kids are all different. A teacher cannot make a student into another student. Sure, you wish all your students could be bright, curious, enthusiastic, and, well, perfect. Guess what? Each student, each child; they are themselves. Our calling is to guide them to be the best "self" they can be. That's what we should be, and that's what we should encourage them to be.

Well taught, Corey.

3 NO THUMBS? NO PROBLEM!

Richard had no thumbs. He had five slender fingers on each hand. No opposable digits. He was a slight young man; only five feet tall and about ninety pounds at age eighteen. He seemed happy enough. We mostly judged that by the expression on his face, because he was totally non-verbal. He wasn't in my classroom, but he was in my Boy Scout troop and I saw him every day at lunch and recess. He observed everyone and everything around him, and was almost ninja-like in his movements. He would be standing next to me one minute, and then the next second, he was on the other side of the playground, but I never saw him run.

Five fingers and no opposing thumbs made practically everything difficult for Richard. Imagine dressing yourself...zippers, buttons, and belts....with no thumbs. To eat, Richard had to lace a spoon through his fingers, in an over/under manner like weaving; same thing with holding a pencil. Go ahead, try it. He had no use for a knife and fork, because he could not eat solid food anyway. Richard was born without a lower jaw, so he could not chew. All his food was pureed in a blender by the school cooks and he ate it with a spoon. Not even the best of school lunches can survive that in an acceptable form.

No thumbs, no lower jaw; neither one of these

obstacles seemed to inconvenience this amazing young man. Richard was truly amazing. The most astounding thing about him, besides his unflappable pleasantness, was his ability to catch flies, bees, and hornets out of mid-air flight. He could literally snatch them while they were flying past him. One of these insects would jet past and Richard would just swoop his hand after it...ZAP....the little critter would be hanging helplessly by their wings, between his second and third fingers. It happened so quickly, I kept wishing for a slow-motion film of it.

He was not born with this skill...he learned it, practiced it, and perfected it. He did not do it to show off, although it sure was entertaining to watch. It seemed to be done for amusement and to fill his time at recess. This was before special playground equipment for handicapped children was available. Richard could not grip the chains from which the swings were suspended. He could not hang onto the merry-go-round or climb up the ladder to the slide. Sitting on the teeter-totter and not being able to hang onto the hand grips would have been dangerous, unless we had tied him on like a cowboy on a rodeo bull. We had tried many times to hold onto him to enable him to do these normal kid activities, but he did not like being held as closely and tightly as was required to be safe. So, he made up his own playground game....bug-catching. He never hurt the ones he caught. Richard always took great care in studying them for a minute or so and then letting them go. I never saw him get stung, either.

What might be the life lesson to be learned here, from this severely physically deformed young man?

For me, the lesson is simple. It's really true; a weakness can be transformed into a strength. A negative can be morphed into a positive. Serious life obstacles CAN be overcome and turned into advantages. Lemons can be made into lemonade.

I do not believe I have ever seen a better example of this in my entire career than Richard. He is a glowing example of taking an obviously distinct and crippling disadvantage, and using it as an opportunity to reframe it and develop an exceptional skill. Even with his significantly diminished intellectual capacities.

Are there students you know who think they have something so horribly wrong with them that it will ruin their lives? Tell them about Richard. Tell them to stop complaining about the school lunch.

4 WANNA SEE MY FRIED EGG FACE?

Troy was a young man with Down syndrome, thick glasses on his perfectly round face, Nordic blond hair, big blue eyes, and a killer sense of comedy. Use your imagination.

Troy had a hard time getting his feet off the floor. He shuffled everywhere, hunched over a little with his arms straight down at his side, and he needed frequent reminders to hold his head up so he could see where he was going. But, Troy was not an "institutional" kid. He lived his life with his parents, and he was an only child. Thus, he was my classroom "preppie". Dressed to the nines every day, well-mannered, always saying his pleases and thank-yous....Troy was a special education teacher's dream student. He loved homework, which was often worksheets with clocks for telling time, or with coins, so he could practice counting money. He carried his "sight word" flashcards around in a fanny pack, so he could practice them if he had a few extra minutes. I actually missed him during the forty-five minutes he was out of my classroom to see the speech therapist twice a week.☐ Most of the other teachers in the building greeted him daily with a hearty "Atta boy, Troy!", and he would reward them with the most infectious smile ever.

This kid was an absolute sunbeam. I have known many

teens with Down syndrome, and as a group they are predictably cheerful, but Troy's positive attitude extended far beyond this stereotype. Many times I watched him as he stopped a peer from exploding into a frustrated temper tantrum, or as he brought an extended crying jag to a dead stop. A droopy, depressed classmate would be laughing hysterically in just a few seconds. Troy's secret was his willingness to do whatever it took to stop the negativity and to inject the sad-sack friend with his personal brand of comedy. Mostly, he accomplished this using only his favorite funny face.

"Hey, ya wanna see my fried egg face?"

That's all it took. Troy would tuck in his lips and bulge out his eyes, posing with a dedicated stare, as he jutted out his chin and then took a quick peek to make sure you were watching.

"Don't it look just like my eyeballs is eggs in a frying pan?"

It CERTAINLY did. His sad/mad/unhappy target's response would always be the same. A loud laugh, another laugh, and then you would have to beg him to stop. If it did not get an immediate response, Troy would put his hands on his hips and march around to everyone who might be nearby and show all of them his fried-egg face. Any person involved in one of these scenarios would be in on the loud laughing within seconds.

This was part of his effectiveness. Troy didn't just get the target person to laugh, he would create a chorus of laughter. And he knew when to quit. At just the right moment, with the timing of a seasoned entertainer, Troy would give a satisfied sigh.

"Now that's a whole lot better. Let's just be happy."

Troy would get back to whatever business he was tending to before his "show". A bad situation had been completely turned around, and Troy would act like nothing had happened.

I truly wish I had a photograph of Troy and his fried-egg face. It was one of those things that just had to be seen in person to get the full effect. Only in one of those moments, could you see the pure joy he felt by being able to help someone laugh when they needed it most. It was his gift.

Troy made it easy to laugh, because he had no problem laughing at himself. He never took the task of making that face seriously. He never worried how silly or strange he might seem to others. People who didn't know Troy might think, "He looks so different already with that funny walk, weird eyes, and thick glasses; why would he make a face like that and make himself look even goofier?"

Why would he do that? He would do that because Troy cared about his friends and not about himself. He was a giver, not a taker. He never complained, argued, or slacked. He had a life to live and a mission to accomplish. Wouldn't it be wonderful to have more folks like Troy in your life?

Troy will always be in my life. He is permanently impressed on my brain. Laugh…life is too short to be unhappy. Don't take yourself so seriously. Smile, who cares how goofy you look…it feels good. And it usually makes the people around you feel good, too. Thanks, Troy.

5 SILENCE IS NOT ALWAYS GOLDEN

Scott was in my classroom for two and a half years. He was one of the first students I had as a special education teacher. Those of you who are teachers know how special that group of kids will always be. You know how you treasure the relationships that develop with them, as you find your way into the world of teaching and they loyally follow you down that path. Even now, many years later, you can recall a cache of the daily exchanges of information, encouragement, disappointments, and mostly wonderful adventures in learning new skills. Good communication skills are very near the top of the list for a rewarding teaching career. Verbal exchanges with children shape every school day.

It was, however, a very long two years into my time with Scott, before he spoke a single word to me. He was fifteen when he came to my room, and before that, he had not uttered a single word to anyone in five years. This part is a hard story to tell. I will try to keep it simple. When he was ten years old, he had been stripped, tied down to a bed, and beaten with a 2x4 by an abusive stepfather. He stopped talking. Horrific trauma will cause that. The diagnosis was that Scott had become what is called an "elective-mute". He simply chose to quit talking. Scott had been taken away from his family, lived unsuccessfully in many foster homes, and was now living in a group home. The perpetrator being in prison was no comfort to Scott; he was damaged for life.

Scott had been a normal ten-year-old, but five years later, he walked into my room as a teenager with the intellectual and emotional development of a ten-year-old. Frozen in time, he came into my classroom; a Level 3 special education class for severely intellectually challenged students. His personality development had been stopped. He had what is called the "walking on eggshells" walk. Every step was slowly considered. It is common in elective mutes. They focus so intensely on not speaking (try it for a day), that their learning grinds to a halt. All their senses are heightened; touch, hearing, etc. His face was very expressive. It was with his smiles and grimaces that he was able to communicate without speaking. He was also able to describe many things with his hands. It was like having a mime in the classroom.

I was supposed to do a complete functional living assessment on him. Can he tell time and do basic counting? Does he know the calendar, how to read, or how to count money? Most of my high school age students were not studying academic subjects, but instead were learning these practical skills that get adults in a sheltered workshop through their day.

It quickly became apparent that testing Scott was going to be a challenge. All his answers had to be in writing. He wrote in the same large primary printing that he probably used as a ten-year-old. If he made any tiny error in his writing, he would erase everything on the page and start over. It was a tedious process, but I finally was able to determine that he already knew pretty much everything that a "graduate" of my classroom should know.

I realized the reason he was placed in my room was because I was the new young teacher; the administration felt that I would have the energy and drive to figure out what really needed to be done with this student. This was in the early 1970's special education era. Individualized Educational Plans (IEPs) were brand new. IEP meetings were unfamiliar and the IEPs were all handwritten. Scott's needs were primarily in the mental health area, not academic, although he was functioning five grades below grade level. I consulted with my principal to let him know I needed help in finding the right resources for Scott's needs, and he set up an appointment for me with a specialist at a large university. She just happened to be in the middle of a research project, where she had managed to find eighty elective mutes from all over the country. Talk about serendipity!

She came to see Scott and brought with her an experimental strategy. Scott was at first encouraged just to blow air out of his mouth, in tiny short puffs. This was extremely difficult for him; he had not been speaking for five years and was unaccustomed to having anything come out of his mouth, even air. She worked with him three days a week, for about an hour each time. It took six months until he was ready to be pushed to more forceful puffs. Scott got pretty good at the harder puffs, and then she gave him a book, Tom Sawyer. He was instructed to make himself comfortable in the closed-in cubicle they were using, and to read the book. This cubicle had wooden walls about half-way up, and then glass, to a total height of about six feet. The glass had been painted black for this project and then a video camera lens was directed through a circle that had been left unpainted. It looked black, and

Scott did not know these sessions were being videotaped as part of the research project. Sometimes I would look through the camera and watch him. He worked well with her and enjoyed the individual attention.

With the book, he climbed under the table that they usually worked at, and sat cross-legged, reading. The researcher asked him to just move his lips as he read, so she knew he was reading. He was not expected to make any sounds. Scott complied with her request and read Tom Sawyer, The Outsiders, several short stories, The Diary of Anne Frank (he cried, silently), and several Hardy Boy mysteries.

This went on for an entire school year and the following summer. The children in our school required a year-round education, and summer school was a much appreciated source of extra income for most of the teachers. It was during the more informal summer school sessions that some of the other students on the playground began to tell teachers that Scott was talking to them. The staff all began to watch Scott more carefully at recess, in the lunchroom, and in the hallways; less structured times when he might be opening up to his peers. No one ever saw him do anything that remotely appeared to be talking to the other students. We eventually decided that the whole student body, mentally challenged as they were, had become aware of the project to get Scott to speak again, but were making up stories, competing to be the one who would first hear him speak.

When school began in the fall, Scott had just finished a book, and wrote me a note saying he was ready for another one. As I was instructed to do by the researcher, I told Scott that there was a new plan; he would be given another book to read, but we were asking him to whisper it as he read it.

He wrote me a note: "I can't", it said. I reminded him of how far he had come in the past year, and assured him that he could whisper if he tried. Scott did try, moving him lips more actively, but he was not able to push any words out. He sat under the table and read three more books, moving only his lips.

Each book, he was encouraged to try to whisper. We modeled whispering. We explained whispering. We began to have other students whisper to each other, to us, and to Scott. It became a game. Christmas came and went. No whispering from Scott, but he was by far the most literate student in our building.

The researcher developed a new strategy; we would require Scott to generalize his lip moving beyond the book reading. Whenever he wanted something, he could no longer write us a note. He had to ask us by moving his lips to 'mouth' the words. He normally had very simple requests, like using the restroom and getting a drink.

It was easy, after working with him for over a year, to know what he was asking without really having to be a lip reader. He had picked up some sign language and finger spelling by watching us work with some of the other non-verbal children, but he wasn't allowed to use those. So, that was how we spent the late winter and early spring months. I became expert at lip reading, at least for Scott's simple requests.

It was during this time that I realized how badly I wanted to be the first one to whom he spoke. He was standing in front of me many times every day, week in and week out, moving his lips, but not talking. It was quite frustrating, but we knew from earlier experiences, anything that looked remotely like frustration or anger would send him to a corner, sitting on the floor, head in his hands, for an hour or more. So his requests were always met with compliance and a smile; with a "Good job, Scott", and he would always smile proudly back at me.

I finished my second school year with Scott, and my second summer with Scott came. With the help of the local council of the Boy Scouts of America, every one of our 200 intellectually challenged students was a Boy Scout. The girls could go to a day camp that we held just outside of the city, but some of the boys were groomed to go to a regular Boy Scout camp in the northern part of the state for two weeks. Scott was selected to go with us. He was now seventeen years old and was a tall, lean young man. He had a sweet smile and a helpful, cheerful attitude; he was a great camper and Boy Scout. Except for his cautious elective-mute style of walking and his complete silence, he appeared to be your average scout.

I had an inkling that Scott really DID want to talk again, but was having a hard time just doing it for the first time. I could tell, after two years with him, when I looked into his eyes, when he mouthed his words to me. Sometimes he would hold his hand lightly in front of his open mouth to see if there was any air coming out. He would look surprised and pleased when he discovered there was. His eyes would widen and it appeared as though he was contemplating what it might feel like if SOUND came out, but it didn't. I felt we were getting so close!

It happened suddenly, early on a Saturday morning at the camp. On Friday night, we had managed to overcook the chicken we were cooking over the campfire. This was to be our dinner, so to the many cries of "It's burned!" I told the scouts, "It's not burned unless it's black on the inside." We ate it and it was burned, but not to the bone. It was black and dry, but those boys were scouts, and they obeyed. Our fried potatoes and apple cobbler were perfect, so no one went to bed hungry.

The next morning, Saturday, it was raining. It was not raining hard, but steadily. The boys had to cook breakfast, as they were working on merit badges with that requirement. None of them wanted to come out of their tents, except Scott. I awakened him first, because he was by far the best fire-builder, and our fire needed some major rebuilding because of the dampness. Scott got it ready for the pre-determined "cooks-of-the-day", but they refused to come out of their tents. As the two of us stood in front of their tents, hearing their "It's raining!" protests, Scott turned to me and whispered very clearly, but in a raspy voice, "Tell them it's not raining unless their underwear is wet." His seven years of silence were over. My eyes were instantly flooded with tears. They are welling as I write this. Then I laughed, and we hugged. I was expecting the clouds to part and a huge double rainbow to appear. That didn't happen, but when I repeated Scott's words to those boys hiding in the tents, they came out instantly.

"Scott just told me, it's not raining unless your underwear is wet!"

Heads popped out of front tent flaps.

He repeated himself, softly whispering, his eyes darting around to make sure everyone was listening, "It's not raining unless your underwear is wet."

They all dashed out into the damp early morning rain

and the rain did seem to let up quite a bit just then. There were hugs all around. These kids were huggers anyway; and this was a hugging occasion, for sure.

Scott whispered a few more times that day, and the following days. We were at wilderness camp, without his therapist, in pre-cell phone days. It was a long hike and quite an ordeal to make a phone call. I decided to wait until we returned home. I could tell he knew he had broken through the wall separating him from the world. I had worked and waited for over two years; pushing him, encouraging him. I had been patient, impatient, optimistic, and pessimistic, but I tried to never let the impatience and discouragement show. Scott did all the hard work though. Who could ever know the thoughts he had for the seven long years that he had been silent? The researcher/therapist said he probably stopped talking because what he had to say about what happened to him at ten was too horrible to tell anyone. With his first utterance at camp, he had revealed a great sense of humor, which had been hidden all those silent years.

Scott had an impact on me, obviously. This tale happened over thirty years ago. What does it mean for me today? What can all teachers learn from this?

Well, as we know too well, horrible things that are too awful to talk about are done to children. Sometimes, rarely, as with Scott, those kids just quit talking. Most of the time, these children act out. They act out at home, or school, or in their neighborhood. We all have them in our classes. I believe that whether they are silent or screaming, we need to listen. Be patient. Encourage them. Smile at them. Give them chance after chance to succeed. We need to get them some professional help. Never give up on anyone. That line has been on my professional business cards for years. NEVER give up on anyone. Sometimes it takes even more than two years, and that seemed like a long time to wait back then when I was a new, young teacher. Doesn't seem like it's a long time at all, now. Never is NOT a long time, when you are a teacher.

6 OVERALLS AND WONDER BREAD

This is about Jeff, but first I must briefly explain the times we were in. I was beginning my special education teaching career in the early 1970s, just as they were "emptying the institutions". Public Law 94-142 decreed that intellectually challenged children were entitled to a free public education. State residential institutions began closing and group homes for those individuals opened everywhere. Many of these students poured into the public school system. End of history lesson; let me tell you what I learned from Jeff, who was a recent transfer into my class from a closed state institution.

Jeff was short, chubby, and charming. He had rosy red cheeks and a big toothy smile with a gate-sized gap in the middle. His buzz-cut flat top hair was bright carrot orange and he had an enormous crop of freckles. That friendly grin was his trademark. Well, that grin, along with his striped overalls. They were a carry-over from his first fourteen years of institutional living. Jeff wore overalls every day. Underneath, he donned either a white t-shirt or a gray cable-knit sweater, depending on the weather.

And then there was that slice of bread. White bread. Wonder Bread; according to Jeff, it was called "Wunnerful

Bwead". A single small slice was stuffed into his centered bib overall pocket, right under his chin. Jeff had an overall-type body. You know, a stout rounder physique that was better suited to a pair of overalls than to a belted pair of pants.

Even though I knew he had a hearty breakfast at the group home before school, Jeff would walk around all morning with his hand held tightly against that pocket.

"Save for later, when I hungry, " he would say, squishing the pocket even more firmly with his pudgy hand and turning halfway around, like he was protecting it from being confiscated. It seemed enough for him to just have it. It was somewhat like a gastronomic security blanket, and it came into play every day around eleven o'clock in the morning. We would be working on telling time or counting money, and Jeff would start trying to unsnap his front pocket.

"Wait. I eat, I work good," Jeff would assure me. I would wait. Jeff would eat. Then he would proceed to "work good". Every time. Every day. It was only an hour before lunch, but Jeff was hungry. He could not focus on his lessons at all when he had a rumbling tummy. It was pointless. The easiest thing to do was just give him a minute and let him have his slice of bread.

This happened at a time in special education when rewards like M&Ms were considered a good reinforcement. Jeff did not want candy. It had to be his magical "Wunnerful Bwead". The bread wasn't a reward for Jeff, it was essential; he was hungry. Trying to interest him in being a student of time or money was pointless when he was hungry.

Think about it for just a minute. Time and money are

two pretty darn important commodities in our lives. If we could have more time and more money, most of us would be thrilled. Jeff had no interest in hearing about either one when he needed something to eat.

Students have come into my class over the past thirty years and not one of them has been the same as another. Each student has been unique and special. However, there has been one common thread they shared with each other, and with any child: if they were hungry, they were unteachable.

As a mother, the thought of a truly hungry child is not acceptable to me, and it is probably not acceptable to you either. I never sent one of my own children to school with an empty stomach, making noises with its own gurgling juices. Who would do that? You would be surprised how regularly it happens. These days, many struggling single moms or dumped-on grandmothers are just lucky to be able to scrape their child out of bed and get them to school in the nick of time.

And there they sit. Stomachs empty. Maybe with a hunger headache to boot, and not the least bit interested in anything happening in my room. Sure, there are free breakfast programs, but sometimes the food is all put away in the lunchroom by the time these tardy, sluggish kids drag themselves through my door.

I feed them. No questions asked. A bunch of bananas lounge on the front edge of my desk every day. Just take one; you really don't have to ask. Any time, all day long. They are not slices of Wonder Bread, but they quell the grumbling tummies and are found on the "approved classroom snack" list. They put kids' minds back in the learning mode, and make them teachable again. I also provide a cooler full of ice water every day. Researchers have shown kids learn better when properly hydrated.

There is simply no point in a teacher trying to work with a hungry child. Jeff taught me this....he could focus on the lesson, but only when his stomach wasn't demanding his already limited attention. Thanks to Jeff and his "Wunnerful Bwead", I also know this: there is a broad spectrum of reasons which might keep a student from being able to learn while in my classroom, but being hungry will NEVER be one. For cryin' out loud, just feed the kids! Bon appetit, Jeff.

PS- This has only a tangential connection to Jeff's story, but I include it to demonstrate that even after all my years in the classroom, I can still have "firsts". Last week I received a girl in my classroom, who has only lived in Des Moines since June. She came from Chicago. She had never even held a real banana in her hand before. She had never tasted one. She had absolutely no experience with bananas in the first fifteen years of her life, beyond seeing them in a pile at the grocery store. (We convinced her to take one small bite. She didn't like it much.) I keep crackers in my desk drawer now, in case she comes in hungry someday.

Nope, I can't make this stuff up!

7 ROSEMARY'S SHOWER

Don't you love the smell of rosemary? It truly is a delicious herb to flavor potatoes, lamb, chicken, and add a distinctive touch to every sort of gourmet dish. It is also a girl's name.

I had a student named Rosemary, but sadly, she did not live up to her namesake seasoning. She came from a family of eight; two parents and six children. All six of the children were intellectually challenged. Back in the 1970s they called it "familial retardation". Genetic failure. I think I would have quit after the second child was diagnosed, but these parents were poor, and mildly intellectually challenged themselves. By the time social services got to them, they had six offspring.

They did the best they could, but the mother and father really had their hands full. The parents always cooperated with school and with the state agencies, so they never took the children away; at least not during the time I knew them.

I was teaching in the mornings and spending the afternoons visiting the families of our students, in their homes. It was a federal project my school had become involved in. We were trying to find out if we could help parents extend the learning the kids did at school into their homes in the evenings. We tried to teach the parents how to help the children practice their new skills at home.

For example, I taught parents how to teach their children the "back-chaining" way to tie shoelaces. If they taught them the same way we did at school, it would hopefully cause less confusion for the child and shorten the time it took them to master that skill. We tried to transfer many skills to the homes in this way. The grant program went for three years, and I felt it was successful.

Well, my task with Rosemary, and with her five siblings, was to teach them how to properly bathe. We did not teach this at school, but every staff person at school knew this was a skill these parents had not taught their children. The six of them were extremely 'fragrant', and not in a good way. Rosemary was sixteen and her hygiene was simply abominable. She had fairly curly and closely trimmed brown hair and for a teen, her skin was relatively free of acne. She was tall, with good posture, and could have presented herself as an average girl, except for that awful odor. I will politely describe it as a sour and biting combination of intense body odor mixed with a urine/feces scent. Rosemary smelled nothing like rosemary.

It was a steamy, early September afternoon when I visited Rosemary's home to explain this new program. The front room appeared to be fairly neat, but not at all clean. It was dark, dusty, and smelled like "dog." I was ushered into the kitchen, where the parents and I sat around a large oval table, where I presumed they ate meals with their large crew of children. It was covered with a clean bright yellow tablecloth. I started explaining my purpose while they smiled and nodded their approval of the idea. They actually wanted me to teach all the children to bathe, stating that they knew they had been having very little luck with their own efforts.

We had only been seated there maybe one minute, and slowly, an extremely foul and rancid odor wafted up to my nose. I leaned a little forward, then a little to the side, and realized it was coming from under the table.

"Do you have a sewer back-up problem?" I asked, even though that was not exactly the right smell.

"Oh no, don't worry about that, the dog had her puppies under the table yesterday. We just haven't had a chance to clean it up yet."

I tried very hard not to gag, and quickly asked if I could see the bathroom. I just wanted to see the tub or shower arrangement they had so I would know how to simulate their bathroom in the locker room at school.

The bathroom was upstairs. The floor was covered with hair, the mirror was small and cracked, and well, I will spare you the condition of the toilet. The tub was filled with dirty clothes; it was overflowing, and piled high, about three feet over the top edge. It was obvious that this tub had not been used in a really long time.

I looked at the mom. Knowing she could probably read the concern on my face, I tried to mask my distress when I asked, "Where do the kids bathe or shower?"

"They just wash up down in the kitchen sink. The faucet up here don't work," she replied, with a helpless shrug of her small shoulders. "The water in the tub works, but I can't catch up on the laundry for all these kids." I arranged with the school social worker to get Mom help catching up on the laundry.

I took Rosemary to the shower at school. We didn't usually instruct kids in bathing; we only used the tub/shower combination to clean up a child if they became ill or incontinent and needed to "start over" before going home. We kept spare clothes there and normally used it only for emergencies.

Rosemary took off her clothes in the restroom stall and came out with a towel around her, as I had asked. I saw she was still wearing her bra, and she seemed genuinely surprised that she had to remove it. When she dropped the towel to remove her bra, I saw she also still had on her underpants. Again, Rosemary really did not know that it was necessary to totally strip before showering. This girl, at age sixteen, had never had a real bath or a shower. She had only done "sponge baths" her entire life. She probably wore her underpants to her "baths" in their kitchen, for modesty reasons.

If you can recall the happiest, most refreshing time you have ever been in the shower; when that water felt so warm and enveloped you in its comforting torrents….multiply that times 1000, and that is the delight Rosemary experienced that day. She used the shampoo sample first, as I instructed her from the other side of the shower curtain. Then, she got her washcloth soaped up and scrubbed herself top to bottom. After washing her private area thoroughly for the first time in her life, Rosemary was somewhat alarmed, as was I, at the fistful of pubic hair in the washcloth. Then she rinsed.

She was a good student. She did the washcloth routine again, and again, and again. She took forty-five minutes and showered four times. I finally had to give her a sixty-second countdown, and then I reached in to turn off the faucets. She stood there and cried, sobbing into her washcloth and begging me to let her do it again. I got her to come out and wrap the towel around her by promising her she could do it again the next day.

We taught all of Rosemary's siblings to shower. A male teacher helped with the two boys, and I taught the three other girls. The parents were so grateful and three months later, the tub at home was still being used regularly. Rosemary was able to get a part-time position in our school's vocational education department's Marriott Hotel housekeeping program. Previously, her poor hygiene had prevented her from being employed. It was a happy ending for everyone. The bus driver who drove those six kids back and forth to school didn't have to spray his bus with Lysol every day. The youngsters started to make more friends at school and every other teacher in the building thanked me repeatedly.

I felt guilty. I had been paid to do something that I was sure I would have done for free. Even if I had not been a teacher, and I discovered this family who did not know how to bathe, I would want to teach them. It was the only humane thing to do. To me, there is something obscene in that kind of uncleanliness. Not pornographically obscene, but the inhumane kind of obscene. In the first twenty-five years of my life, even living on a farm, I had never seen that kind of filth. In the forty years I have lived since then, I have not seen it again. It was appalling, and I fixed it. It was so simple, really, and the simplicity of it still astounds me. It felt SO good to have helped those kids, and it was so easy. All it took was a little soap and water.

I think everyone should have something that horrifies them to the point of taking action to remedy it. I want everyone to have that feeling that I experienced when I taught Rosemary to bathe herself. I'm not talking about trimming your toenails when they get too long. I'm not talking about dropping some change in a red Salvation Army bucket. Of course, we all need to do those necessary and those generous things to be human and to share our bounty with others. What I am aiming at is the idea of correcting something that cannot be allowed to exist.

Everyone can fill in their own blank. You each can name something whose existence is intolerable to you. Go do something to change it. Try to help fix it. Think big. It could be something that would benefit just one person. It could be global, but it doesn't have to be; just so it makes someone's world better. It doesn't have to the whole world. Go get your 'soap and water' and get busy.

8 FRANKENSTEIN OR JAWS

Wearing a red plaid flannel shirt and a pair of men's jeans, Lida stepped hesitantly into my classroom. Her Afro was trimmed quite close. With her straight up and down physique, she could have been mistaken for a boy. I welcomed her warmly, but she neither looked directly at me, nor did she return my smile. She didn't want to sit down, choosing instead to stand in the far back corner the entire first day of school. She was correctly placed in my room, I knew that for sure.

At sixteen, this sad-eyed bi-racial girl never used makeup, but always wore a long-sleeved flannel shirt and jeans. It was like her uniform. She cooperated well with instruction and was actually a very bright young woman. Of course, in my class, bright was always a relative term. The rest of my students were there for the same general reason: each one was normal or near normal intellectually, but functioned at a level that put them in the range of being severely developmentally disabled. To put it another way, they were mentally ill or had another condition that prevented them from performing at their maximum level of intelligence. They were not regular high school material. I called my classroom the "junior college" of our special school for intellectually handicapped kids.

Like many of the others, Lida had been traumatized. At first, the social worker was very obtuse about exactly what had happened to her. She dodged my occasional inquiries with comments like, "It really won't help you to know", and "You should speak with her mother about that." Even these days, with my current students, I generally do not make it a practice to know all the gruesome details of their lives. Too much information can make it difficult to be the fair-handed educator, instead of their therapist. I decided to wait until parent conference time in the fall, and just cover the topic with her mother then.

I discovered the extent of damage to Lida the third day of school. The building principal was "making his rounds" and he knocked on my classroom door, peeking through the window in the door. Because she had insisted that she did not want anyone sitting behind her, Lida was seated in the back of the room, near the bank of windows on my east wall. Seeing his mustached face and hearing his first three or four firm knocks, Lida jumped out of her desk, nearly knocking it over. She extended her arms at shoulder level out in front of her and started growling; then she began pacing back and forth in front of the windows, marching with large stiff steps, like Frankenstein. The effect she was aiming for was perfectly obvious. She never took her eyes off the door. The "monster" was on guard in the rear of my class.

Dr. H., my principal, was a sweet older Pakistani gentleman. He had a developmentally disabled son of his own and was very loving and gentle toward all the students. He heard the loud noises coming from my room and opened the door.

Lida shouted, "You need to leave! Frankenstein is angry and dangerous! Get out!"

Dr. H. knew exactly what to do. He backed out and

37

closed the door behind him. Lida completed stomping two more lengths of the classroom and returned to her seat; then she crossed her arms on top of the desk and put her head down. I just stood there, not moving or speaking, while this thirty second drama played itself out. The other students resumed their lessons.

A similar incident occurred two days later. A male custodian came into the room to examine our wall of windows for their winter readiness.

This time, Lida abruptly stood up again, then backed a few steps into the corner of the room, with a fixed stare at the man. She put one of her hands on each side of her mouth and started clasping her fingers in chomping motions, while simultaneously making loud chomping sounds with her own teeth. In a low, almost bass rumbling voice, Lida warned, "Look out for Jaws! Look out for Jaws!" Her eyes were fierce, but also fearful.

The custodian retreated to the hall, just as the principal had, saying he would be back after school. Lida returned to her seat, and put her head down for a while. The movie Jaws had been released the previous summer and most of my students had seen it. They were very complimentary about Lida's shark simulation, but she did not thank them. It was serious business for her, not entertainment. We had episodes like this less than once a week after Lida became more familiar with the male adults in the building. The females caused no alarm for her, but any unknown man she saw sent her into her Jaws or Frankenstein terror. At outside recess, I had to make sure she did not venture too close to the six-foot high chain link fence that surrounded out downtown school playground. An unsuspecting man passing by on the sidewalk could trigger one of these episodes. She would still get that fearful wide-eyed look when around the familiar men, but not resort to the scary imitations. Her purposeful androgynous appearance provided some cushion for her; many folks thought she was a boy.

At fall parent conferences, Lida's mother came at the scheduled time. We usually wanted to have students at the conferences, but her mom had left Lida at home. When I joined this mother at the conference table, she already had tears rolling down her face. The social worker had her arm around Lida's mother and was comforting her. Smiling at me and patting the mother's shoulder, the social worker assured me that these tears were tears of joy. She was so happy Lida was staying in school, making friends, and not resisting attendance.

"After all she has been through," Mom finally explained, "she deserves to feel safe and happy. I know she will never be the same after this rape, but I am willing to do whatever it takes to make her feel protected.

Why hadn't the social worker told me at the beginning of the school year that Lida had been raped? I had thought all along that the root of her behavior was probably rape, or some other sort of sexual assault. Within the first week of school, I had seen Lida transform herself into two impervious characters in the presence of unknown men. She was afraid of most men and her adaptive behavior was to transform herself into those extremely frightening creatures. Pretty clever, really. Who is less vulnerable than Jaws or Frankenstein? Obviously, this reaction seems a little extreme, even for a rape. Rape is horrific crime, and Lida had been raped horrifically, by several men, several times. Lida had lost herself. She was so full of hurt and sadness. Our experts found that her mental disability made it difficult to counsel her. Still, she had found her own way to defend herself.

As the conference proceeded, I was able to report glowingly on Lida's progress in all areas of her academics and behavior. She was indeed making friends and making good gains in her life skills. Her grooming had improved greatly, although she still insisted on her flannel shirt and jeans wardrobe.

One of her best friends from my class was a very hyperactive young man. He was a slim, blond, blue-eyed talking machine. Lida never tired of listening to him. He was so grateful to have her for a friend. They also lived in the same neighborhood, so they became fishing buddies in the local creek. Their weekend jaunts to the banks of that creek gave them both much pleasure, until one fateful Saturday. The young man decided to bring his two brothers with him. They had no ill intent; they just wanted to meet Lida.

When he went to meet Lida down by the creek, she observed them approaching her. She apparently felt trapped between them and the creek, so as they approached, in spite of the fact that her good friend Bobby was with them, Lida pulled out a pocket knife. She stabbed her friend three times and each of his brothers twice, before she ran away. They were superficial wounds, but the damage had been done. There was more damage coming Lida's way. The police were called and when they came to her house to arrest her, there was a ferocious struggle by some very tenacious police officers before they were able to handcuff the terrified Frankenshark. Lida was hospitalized after threatening suicide in juvenile detention.

Ultimately, the young men and their parents did not

press charges, and it was not even the end of the fishing friendship. However, the part of this narrative that does not turn out happily is the additional trauma inflicted on Lida. She had been traumatized by the fright of possibly being gang-raped again. Her arrest was a tragically violent one. She had unfortunately wounded a gentle young man she felt true friendship toward. The young man's forgiveness did not comfort Lida. Having her mother accompany them on future fishing trips really took away the sense of independence and adventure that was most of these excursions' appeal. Most importantly, Lida's sense of personal safety had once again been devastated. It was a very dark time for her.

Lida was in my classroom for three more years. She made tremendous strides in her life during that time. She became an assistant for feeding one of the most severely handicapped younger students in our building. She excelled in her home economics classes. Lida also helped a volunteer from a nearby dental college organize an after-lunch tooth brushing program for all 200 students in the school. At nineteen she transitioned into the vocational part of our curriculum and became trained as a housekeeper at a suburban Marriott hotel. Her mother "teamed" with her and they were allowed to work together. It gave Lida the independence of her own paycheck, while letting her work with the physical security of a trusted partner. By this time, the days of Jaws and Frankenstein were behind her. Maybe not far behind her, but intentionally pushed into the past. She was determined to move forward.

Lida was what I call a "long-term project". There were times, like the stabbing, when it seemed like Lida's life was on the edge of complete ruin. Still, she persevered, far beyond her limited mental capacity. This accomplishment, in itself, is almost unbelievable.

My lesson from this was simple. Redemption exists. Coming from an experience that would put most adult women into years of therapy, this teenager survived multiple subsequent traumas, and still prevailed. I do not know what reaching the "lowest point" might be for a teenage girl, but I think Lida must have been close, more than once. She battled back from rape. She struggled with suicidal thoughts. She overcame immobilizing, irrational fear. Certainly, her coping mechanism was not a conventional one, but Frankenstein and Jaws gave her space and time to recover her sanity and find her way to her future. I want to believe that the adult Lida is happy, working, maybe still living with her mother; maybe even still friends with Bobby. I am sure she is surrounded by loving, caring family and supporters, and that she is helping others, volunteering, giving back, and feeling appreciated. She deserves that.

9 MACK TRUCK! MACK TRUCK! MACK TRUCK! MACK TRUCK!

I was a brand new teacher. My newly-born pedagogical skills still had placental blood on them. It was my first year and I was in a room with fifteen mentally-disturbed and intellectually challenged teenagers. I was in survival mode. Oh, for sure, I ate determination for breakfast every morning, snacked on little bites of encouragement for lunch, but I drank a half bottle of wine the minute I walked into my house at 4:30PM every afternoon. I usually didn't even take off my coat or pour the wine into a glass. I just walked in the front door, went straight to the refrigerator, popped the cork, and drank it out of the bottle. Chateau Ste. Roseline. My own children ate a lot of Spaghettios that first year of teaching.

The subjects of the previous chapters, Jeff, Lida, Rosemary, Troy, Scott, Mark, and Corey, were all in my classroom at the same time. And so was Bobby. Bobby was Lida's non-stop talking fishing friend in the previous chapter.

This chapter is about Bobby. He was medicated with the gold standard of hyperactivity-battling medication back then in the early 1970s....Ritalin. It didn't even faze him. Well, maybe it did, but I never saw him in the evenings, when it probably wore off. I only know for certain that it did not slow his speech down at all during the school day. He was the quintessential "motor mouth". I label him with that only in the most affectionate possible manner. He never used foul language and was always in a chipper mood. Bobby just never stopped talking. He couldn't help it, so that made the non-stop nature of it much less annoying than you would think, but much of it was nonsense. I suspect Bobby wasn't even sure why he said most of the things that came out of his mouth.

One day, almost everything Bobby talked about was related to trucks. My two teacher associates and I had listened to him most of the morning. Even with him doing most of his talking from his "office", behind a sound-proofed room divider, we had reached our saturation point. Our other students had also heard enough. We all just needed a couple of minutes of peace. I asked Bobby if he would please just stand out in the hall for five minutes....maybe he'd like to be our classroom policeman...."stand guard" at the door. There were windows in the door, so I could still observe him. Well, Bobby was very interested in this opportunity, but was sure he would need someone to talk to while he was out there. Being such a clever first-year teacher, I thought of the lockers in the hallway...the ones with the ventilation slots across the top of them. I suggested to Bobby that he could just "talk to the lockers". What a great solution! "Pretend those air slots are a microphone! It will be fun, Bobby."

Assigning Bobby to the hall for five minutes seemed like a wonderful idea for everyone. The other students could have a brief quiet time of respite, and the classroom staff could get a few minutes to gather our thoughts before moving to the next activity. Bobby could free-lance verbalize with unfettered freedom.

What could possibly go wrong?

I did not calculate the possibility of the principal showing up. Sure enough, as I found out later, after Bobby had been out in the hall only a minute, there was our school principal, Dr. H., strolling down the third floor hallway.

And there was Bobby, speaking in his fast-paced well-articulated voice, yapping into the locker..."Mack Truck! Mack Truck! Mack Truck! Mack Truck!" .....pause.... "Mack Truck!Mack Truck! Mack Truck! Mack Truck!"...pause...."Mack Truck! MackTruck! Mack Truck! Mack Truck!".....and on and on and on.

"Oh! Hi, Dr. H.! Mack Truck! Mack Truck! Mack Truck! Mack Truck!"

"Hello, Bobby. What are you doing out here?"

"My teacher sent me out here. She said I can be the class policeman. She said I could talk to the locker. Mack Truck! Mack Truck! Mack Truck! Mack Truck!"

"Bobby, how long have you been out here?"

"Only a little time, sir. I only have five minutes! Mack Truck! Mack Truck! Mack Truck! Mack Truck!" ...pause...."Mack Truck! Mack Truck! Mack Truck! Mack Truck!" ...pause...."Mack Truck! Mack Truck! Mack Truck! Mack Truck!"

I peeked out the window to see how Bobby was doing. He was doing great. Talking to the locker. Having a wonderful time. I went back to the rest of the class for another couple of minutes, and then beckoned Bobby back into the room.

The rest of our morning was a little quieter. All that "locker talk" had worn Bobby out a bit. The afternoon went uneventfully, the short yellow buses came to take the kids home, and it was quiet on the third floor.

I went to the second floor, to the main office, to check my teacher mailbox. Seeing me from his office, Dr. H. called to me, "Terri, please come talk with me."

He had a thick Pakistani accent, but I have become accustomed to it. I loved the way he said the word "discipline". It sounded like "dah sip' a lin". He had several children of his own who were doctors and lawyers, as well as his youngest son, who was intellectually challenged. Dr. H. had been a well-known entomologist in his native country, but when this son was born, he re-entered the university, earned another doctorate in special education, and brought his family to America. He was a remarkably gentle, caring school administrator.

Fortunately, he liked me. He used to tell me that he hired me because I looked like the actress Raquel Welch. I have no idea how that was possible, since she is a brown-eyed brunette, and totally exotic-looking. I was a blond, blue-eyed Iowa farm girl, but I was flattered nonetheless. However, he always made me feel he respected my teaching ability and he gave me many leadership opportunities within our school.

So, that day...the day of Mack Truck....I entered his office and sat down across the desk from him. He was smiling broadly and shaking his head from side to side.

The conversation went something like this, "Terri, you are a good teacher and a strong teacher. You are a smart woman. You do miracles with your students every day. This morning I found Bobby in the hall, talking to the locker."

I didn't know he had been out there. I quickly tried to tell him why I had left Bobby in the hall by himself, "I can explain. The whole classroom needed a little break. It was only for five minutes. Bobby had a good time out there."

"I'm glad it worked out today, but I think I have a better idea. Please call me when your class needs a break. I will listen to Bobby for a few minutes. I have plenty of time and would be happy to help you. Call me, please. I enjoy Bobby; he's a good boy." Then he added, "Why don't you go home early? You've had a long day."

That great man has been the standard I have used to judge every administrator I have worked for since then. He cared for the kids. He cared for the teachers. He put his personal touch on every part of our school. I will never forget that man, who taught me to ask for help if I need it. He taught me to take a break when I need it.

Then there is Bobby, who taught me to give my students a break when they need it, or when I need it. He also taught me there are ideas that seem to be good at first, but are not always that good. In the future, however, Bobby did get more breaks in the hall, with Dr. H. They enjoyed each other, and my classroom enjoyed a few minutes of peace and quiet.

Thanks, Dr. H., and thanks, Bobby.

10   THE SALAD MELTDOWN LESSON

Kathy was an extremely angry, explosive teenage girl. She was sixteen and tiny; just 4'10" tall. She was perfectly proportioned, very curvaceous, and she really, really, really liked attention from boys. She had classic Norwegian coloring: blonde hair, blue eyes, and creamy white skin. Kathy was quite pretty, intellectually challenged, and mentally ill. We struggled daily with her wardrobe, which was always sexually provocative, and with her makeup, which was always more appropriate for clubbing than for school. She had a sweet little bell-like voice and could be delightfully charming. When she became angry, the screams that came out of her mouth could shatter wine glasses. Her second language was profanity.

My classroom had been moved from the special school where I taught, to a regular city high school. My students were the highest functioning in the special program, so we were selected to "transition" for the purpose of normalizing their social skills. None of them had academic skills high enough to include in the regular classes, but we were to be in the hallways, the lunchroom, and the physical education classes with the other students. Hindsight has told me it was a huge miscalculation to include Kathy in this project.

The first indication that Kathy was going to have difficulty came at the end of the initial week of our inclusion in the school. I was called to the counselors' office on Friday afternoon. Miss Elliot, the lead counselor, informed me there were several accounts from young men who had their rear-ends pinched in the hallways near our classroom. The reports were all similar: the boys felt a pinch as they were walking, and when they turned around, they saw a short blonde girl running away. Guess who?

I was not surprised, but I pretended to be. I had talked, explained, role-played, and "laid down the law" with Kathy for weeks before we left the security of Emerson. She knew better, but she simply could not help herself when it came to touching the boys. There had been one or two pinching incidents in my room before, but she was not very earnest about going after the boys in my class. Most of them looked handicapped, and she was not at all interested in them as boyfriend material. She had created her fantasy sweetheart from photos in the magazine Seventeen. Being in this regular school, full of normal red-blooded boys, football players, basketball players, and wrestlers, was a male smorgasbord for Kathy.

The counselor and I spoke with Kathy the following Monday morning. No more hallway pinching. Her reward would be that she could continue to be in the hall during passing time. Her negative consequence, if the incidents continued, was loss of hallway time. She agreed. Monday, there were no incidents; Tuesday, there were no incidents. Wednesday afternoon, I was summoned to see Miss Elliot again. There had been four more reports of fanny-pinching....this time in the lunchroom.

I promised the counselor I would talk with Kathy again, and she would not be eating in the lunchroom or using the hallways during passing times until we had the pinching under control. I had no idea how long that would be. Kathy was basically "grounded" to our room. She was not happy.

"I need to see the boys! I need to see the boys!" she whined and argued. "I promise I won't do it anymore!" she added, stomping her feet several times, like she was putting out a fire, and adding a string of expletives.

I explained that she and I would eat lunch together in our room on Thursday and Friday. Then we would talk about her going to the lunchroom, under supervision, the next Monday. Rumors about "a crazy little blonde chick" were flying around the school. We needed to lower our profile for a few days.

Kathy wanted a salad for lunch and said she wanted Ranch dressing. My classroom associate went to the lunchroom to get the salad, brought it back to the room, and set it on my desk while Kathy and I were in the restroom washing our hands. We came back to the room. My associate had gone to take her lunch break, and I placed Kathy's salad on her desk. All hell broke loose.

The associate had mistakenly gotten French dressing. Ranch/French...it was easy to see how there could be a misunderstanding, especially with the way Kathy had been whining about having to eat in the room.

The high-pitched screeching started. "I neeeeeeeeed Raaaannnnnnccchh! I don't want no fu#%*g French! I neeeeeeeeed Raaaannnnnnccchh!" I tried to calm her. I put my arm around her, but she started crying.

"Kathy, Dorothy thought you said French. I'm sorry. You are going to have to either eat salad with French, or eat the salad without dressing." There was no way I could take her to the lunchroom, in the condition she was in, and I couldn't go get Ranch dressing and leave her in the room alone. This was in pre-cell phone days.

There was absolutely no consoling her. Her voice went higher and higher.

"I neeeeeeeed Raaaannnnccchh! I don't want no fu#%*g French! I neeeeeeeed Raaaannnnccchh!"

She got louder and louder. She threw herself on the floor. I moved the desks out of the way when she started rolling around and kicking her feet and pounding her clenched little fists on the wooden floor. She was shrieking, crying pitifully, cussing, screaming for Ranch dressing, and was totally out of control. Tears were streaming down her bright red face. I could see no way of stopping this. That tiny girl was making an enormous ruckus about Ranch dressing.

A few teachers peeked in the door, but I waved them out again. No one needed to see her like this. My classroom associate, Dorothy, heard what was going on in our classroom, so she picked up our other students from the lunchroom and took them outside for a walk.

Kathy kicked, pounded, shrieked, and cried for thirty minutes. I went to my desk after about ten minutes and turned on the tape recorder. I had never seen or heard anything like this. It was like a really bad tantrum a small child might have, and then fall asleep sobbing. That is exactly what Kathy did; after a half hour, she fell asleep on the floor. Salad untouched. Teacher astounded. Student asleep.

I went to the door, motioned for a passing student, and sent her to go get the school nurse to come to my room. The nurse brought a blanket and a pillow. We gently moved Kathy, who awakened only momentarily, to a cot in the back of the room. She was soaking wet with sweat. We covered her with the blanket, I pulled our portable room divider around the cot, and Kathy slept soundly for the rest of the afternoon. The other students returned and we finished our classes for the day.

When she awoke, she remembered very little of what had happened at lunch. She said she was hungry and ate her salad, with no dressing. Instead of putting her on the special school bus, I drove her home. All the way to her house, she repeatedly apologized for pinching boys. She didn't really recall what had happened at lunch, but she thought it had to do with her pinching boys. She said she didn't like the way she felt...not being able to remember what happened. I didn't tell her everything she did, thinking it was best not remembered.

I did tell her she was going to be eating lunch in the room on Friday and she was fine with that. I had to write an incident report. I played the tape I had recorded for Dr. H., my special school principal.. He looked so sad as he listened to just a minute or two of it. He understood there was no comforting her. Dr. H. said he was sorry I had to experience that, and he was especially sad for Kathy.

Kathy's Friday lunch was uneventful; she and I started repairing our relationship. We talked about how touching boys was not a good idea. It was not what girls did at school. We sat together in the lunchroom all the next week and watched the other girls in the school. We observed no girls pinching boys, and really very little other touching. Kids still had boundaries then.

Kathy returned to the halls and the lunchroom without incident. Just to be sure, my associate followed her, at a distance, for about a month, and Kathy did just fine.

We never discussed the tantrum over Ranch dressing after that. That dressing was really not part of the equation. But, it certainly wasn't the pinching issue that set it off either. What it was is one of the most horrific classroom incidents in all of my years of teaching.

About three months after this happened, shortly after Christmas Break, the school social worker discovered that Kathy was being sexually abused by a sixteen year old stepbrother. It had been going on for almost two years. He was prosecuted and sent to a juvenile institution.

Well, that explained a lot; her overtly-sexual behavior, her low frustration level, and her memory loss. The school psychologist said that the "salad meltdown" she had was probably a mechanism to help Kathy vent her feelings about the abuse.

Kathy was a tough little girl. She was a tragic victim. She had survived her trauma admirably, given her limited intellectual ability. She deserved so much better. Her response to counseling was positive, but there is never a good outcome when a child like Kathy is abused like that.

I have more recently taught in a gender-specific classroom with only female students, and I am still learning. My girls are strong/fragile. Intelligent/gullible. Brave/vulnerable. They have all had trauma of various kinds in their young lives. Most suffer from depression and some are bi-polar. We press on together, looking for their future. I try to teach them to be prepared for whatever opportunities may be presented to them in the years ahead. Their caseworkers, counselors, and therapists provide tremendous support for them and their families, and for me. I have not had anything close to a "salad meltdown" with any of them, but we do still have our "moments".

We tell the girls that whatever "issues" they bring to the room, we will help them deal with them. I strive to foster a positive and nurturing learning environment.

What I learned from Kathy is part of this nurturing. I now know that a student may have an obvious disability (usually a behavior disability in my room), but that disability is not necessarily their biggest problem. A student might say that "this" is what is wrong, but it may really be "that", and they might not even realize it themselves....so how are the adults supposed to figure it out? Hmmmm, I guess that's why I can't wait to get to school every morning.

11 I'M GOING TO MARRY JEFF AND WE'RE GOING TO GET A POODLE

Wendy.

I had two young children of my own when Wendy was in my class. Her name and her personality reminded me of the mother in Peter Pan. My Wendy was a responsible, older-soul type of "mother hen" student. If you are a teacher, you know the kind. They want to make everything OK for everyone, all the time. You always get to check the boxes on their progress report: "good relationships with peers" and "good relationships with adults". Except for Wendy's significant intellectual challenges, I might have hired her to babysit for my kids.

Wendy did not look like a special education student in any way. She was average height and weight. She had medium length, curly brown hair and brown eyes. If you had seen her on the street, you would never have suspected she had serious mental challenges. She had a sprinkle of freckles on her full pink cheeks and a few across her nose. She was a pretty girl.

If she had been a regular high school girl, Wendy would have been an honor student, a cheerleader, and on the student council. In addition to all that, she probably would have played a sport or two and been in the band; probably a volunteer at the local nursing home, also. Wendy was high energy and all smiles. This made it all the more difficult when she would slam down on the floor in a full-blown grand mal seizure.

More than a few students at our school had epilepsy. In this special school, I would estimate about 10-15% of the student body had this condition. Most had it pretty much under control. Now, in the 21st century, the field of medicine has improved medication tremendously and has even developed surgery that can help. Wendy's epilepsy was not very well controlled. She usually had one or two seizures every week. She did not like to wear the standard helmet to protect her skull, but knew it was the rule, so she followed it. My classroom was on the third floor and I was always afraid she might have a seizure while we were on the stairs, so I stayed close to her on the way up and down.

Wendy was a good student. I taught her how to count money, make change, write her name in cursive, and how to tell time. She made a bed like a professional maid and did as well in woodshop class as any of the boys. She excelled in the home economics program; at the age of sixteen she was allowed to help the school cooks as a kitchen helper. Wendy would not need to be in a sheltered workshop the rest of her life. She was headed toward a career in a minimally-supervised normal work situation. She always said she wanted to get married, and had even picked out her man, another student named Jeff. They rode the same yellow bus and Jeff liked her, too. Wendy hoped they could have a nice apartment and get a poodle.

Sadly, none of this was meant to be. I am putting all

the blame on epilepsy. This does not have a happy ending.

It was sudden and abrupt. Wendy was not at school that day. Dr. H. called me to the office. No more Wendy. She had a seizure in her sleep. It couldn't be helped. No one was with her. Wendy choked and died. I returned to my classroom.

When one of your young students dies, a teacher is devastated. It is a totally helpless feeling. It is terribly sad, and frustrating, and the loss is felt for a long time. As one of "your" students, they become a part of your life. You mourn, but you must carry on for your other students.

Wendy was the first of my students to pass away. Over the span of my teaching career, so far, there have been five others. Curtis also died of a seizure. Brad committed suicide. So did Kenny. Lynn and Jerome died in tragic car accidents. I'll never forget them. When I think about Wendy, and these boys, with their stories cut so short, I'm still so very sad.

12   MY FIRST MUSLIM

"I led a very sheltered life", is what I tell people all the time. I say it because I grew up on a farm, my parents were extremely protective, and I attended a small high school (with about 300 total students.) The only minority student was a boy who was one-half Native American. My total environment was pretty much controlled. I was not allowed to date until I was sixteen. Boys were carefully screened, and strict guidelines were enforced. I had the same circle of friends since kindergarten, and the wildest parties I ever attended were my own slumber parties. Sure, I went to downtown Des Moines, such as it was in the middle of the twentieth century, but only on Saturday mornings and under the close supervision of my mother and older sisters. Let's just say, it was a VERY sheltered existence.

When I went to college, at seventeen, I was allowed to live in the dormitory, but my parents had arranged for it to be the smallest dormitory on a campus that was only fifteen minutes away from my home. I was picked up for church every Sunday morning.

At college, however, they really had nothing to say about the people I met. I had been taught by my mother to love all people. My father had a generous portion of ethnic biases. The bottom line is, I was simply not aware of the variety of people who were living on the planet with me. A girl from Hawaii lived across the hall from me. I met my first Bostonian. He was Catholic, which had been taboo for me to date in high school, so it was kind of exciting to have him ask me out on a date. He was a terrible kisser and I could barely understand what he was saying, so we only had two dates. The same was true with the young man from Africa. He was pretty easy to understand, but when he asked me to marry him after three dates (and we had NOT kissed), I knew I had overextended my emerging reach for diversity.

So, I dated a few more guys and by the middle of my junior year in college, I finally settled on one to marry. We married and a few years later, after finishing college and living in several different states, we settled in Minnesota. It was a Lutheran haven, which pleased my parents, and I started my teaching career. My first year of teaching, I made my first openly gay friend, Tim. I had a classroom associate who was Lakota Sioux.

My principal, Dr. H., was my first Muslim. I adored him, even after I personally observed him cheating on his golf score. It was really the only character flaw I found in him in the nine years I taught at his school.

Dr. H., or "Saj", as he wanted us to call him, was totally devoted to helping intellectually-challenged kids. He was in charge of our special school, which educated about 200 severely handicapped students. He originally had a doctorate in entomology and came to the United States to study agriculture, but when his youngest son was born with Down syndrome, Saj obtained his doctorate in special education and administration. He was determined to improve the quality of education for all students with special needs. Saj was from Pakistan and had his quirky pronunciations of English words. My favorite was discipline, which he pronounced as "dah sip ah lin". He knew it was wrong, but eventually just gave up ever trying to get it right.

Saj faithfully observed Ramadan, which is the Muslim holy month when there is no eating or drinking from sunrise to sunset for 29-30 days. He made no big fuss over it. He was a humble man, and extremely patient with his young staff of teachers and associates. When I saw him at the shopping mall, his traditionally-dressed wife was dutifully walking the prescribed ten feet behind him the whole time. However, on the golf course, Saj and I walked side-by-side down the fairway.

One time, Saj was in an awful car crash and had to have some surgery around his mouth. He walked around school holding either a newspaper or a folded white handkerchief in front of his mouth for more than a month, so none of us had to look at the mess on his face. He didn't want to make anyone feel uncomfortable or uneasy.

Saj always worked extremely hard to get us all the resources we needed for our students. He personally helped get Boy Scout uniforms for nearly fifty handicapped Scouts. He made sure "Santa" had nice gifts for all the students and all the staff at Christmas. He regularly brought us delicious treats from his home, always proud to tell us what a wonderful cook and loving mother his wife was. All of his five children, except the youngest, were doctors or college professors.

I know Muslims are extremely suspect for many people these days. I understand. I just know that the first

Muslim I knew personally was a wonderful, gentle, humorous man. When he walked through the halls at school or into my classroom, I felt his fatherly presence watching over us. I worked with him every day for nine years. I know there are extremists, who are dangerous. Saj would never have hurt a fly.

Cheat on his golf score...yes, he did...but I imagine it was only because he thought he might lose to a girl, which probably had more to do with him being a man than being a Muslim.

13   FAILING AS A TEACHER

This is about how one of my biggest failures as a teacher turned into one of the most important lessons I ever learned.

I'm not sure everyone understands what is actually taught when you teach severely intellectually-challenged students. What I thought I was supposed to be teaching my students thirty years ago was simply very elementary or pre-school skills. Shoe tying, counting, colors, telling time, counting money, days of the week, months of the year, writing their own name and address, and basic Dolch List words (sight words and safety words, like: big, little, he she, danger, stop, closed, exit, etc.). I also taught grooming and self-care skills, like brushing teeth, nail care, applying deodorant, matching clothing, and hair care. We taught manners: please, thank you, excuse me, how to use the elevator and how to ride the city bus. Instruction also covered how to answer a phone, including copying down a phone number to call back. Remember, these things could not be taught just once, and then we'd move on to the next skill. Everything had to be demonstrated, modeled, and repeated many, many times, and then taught in various settings, so the skills could be "generalized" to different situations. That was one of the hardest parts. One of the statistics we used then was, "Tell the other kids fifteen times; tell one of our kids forty-five times."

I had a rambunctious student, Eric, who was fifteen years old, and an eager learner. He had prematurely white hair, cut in an old-style flat top. Eric wore thick Coke-bottle like glasses that were so heavy he was always having to push them up; even having a heavy black strap securing them around the back of his head did not prevent them for being down at the end of his nose most of the time.

This young man was motivated to be employed. Someone had thoroughly impressed the benefits of having a job on him, and Eric really wanted to "get to work" as soon as possible. He even walked like he was on his way to a job he couldn't wait to get to; he strode everywhere with purpose. His functioning level, unfortunately, was going to put him in a sheltered workshop. Those workshops were reserved for students who had reached the age of eighteen. Eric had a few years to wait.

Because he simply did not yet understand the calendar, the months, and the years, Eric asked almost every day "how soon" he would be able to go to work. He accepted the answer, "As soon as you get everything on this Working Skills Checklist checked off."

Eric would always reply, "Then let's get busy!"

He was making steady progress on his counting and money skills. Telling time was going to be more difficult, but would be easier once he improved his number skills. After all, we had nearly three more years to work on it. However, the terribly difficult hurdle for Eric on that checklist was learning his basic colors.

Most four year old children know their colors. All we expected was red, blue, green, yellow, orange, purple, pink, white, black, and brown. We started in September. Eric struggled mightily. He would scratch his head, shake his head, and even pound his forehead, while thumbing through all the photographs and color cards. We would play easy matching games; pairing color cards with objects and word cards. Eric could not even match the word "red" with a red circle and a red apple.

He had learned only the sight words for red, blue, green, yellow, and orange by Halloween. Two months into the school year and I had taught him only five color words, and none of the colors. This was disappointing, but I did not let Eric in on my frustration. We met every day with high energy and encouraging words. "You are going to learn all these colors, Eric, and then we will have a color party!"

In the meantime, we played every game and used every visual and tactile strategy in the arsenal of the occupational therapist at school. Colors and Eric did not mix.

Then, the first weekend in November, I drove to the house of a friend, who was a fellow teacher. Her neighbor was having a very late-season garage sale. As my teeth chattered, I started poking through a stack of the neighbor's old Discover magazines. One of them had an article on color-blindness. I jokingly said to my friend, "Maybe this is Eric's problem!"

I bought the magazine and took it to the school nurse on Monday morning. She ran over to the school district offices and borrowed a test kit from the Nursing Supervisor. She would get Eric right after lunch and test him. The color test used numbers and shapes, hidden in pictures that had different colored bubbles in them.

64

Sample test item....Can student see the red square and/or yellow circle?

Eric knew his shapes, but he could not find the square or the circle. He failed the test. He had Deuteranopia, a type of color blindness is characterized by loss of green vision and color distortion in the red-green-yellow part of the spectrum. The red and yellow "bubbles" appeared to be the same color as the rest of the bubbles. Almost everything Eric looked at appeared to be either brown, muddy gold, or tan.☐ He could detect a few shades of dull or dark blue.

Red looked like camouflage green, bananas looked tan, grass appeared to be brown or gold. This made me the most sad for him...can you imagine never seeing green grass? Poor Eric.

So, I had spent (wasted) all of September and October, two whole months of Eric's education, trying to teach color identification to a colorblind student. I felt like a complete idiot, and utterly ineffective as a teacher. Now, in hindsight, I can chalk it up to my youth and inexperience, but it does not diminish the obvious failure of my instincts. We switched gears. Eric had to learn to compensate for not being able to see colors; no amount of remedial instruction was going to teach him his colors. Instead of labelling colors, Eric needed to be able to identify items by size, shape, function, and texture. ☐ "Bring me the book with the kitten on the front", not "Bring me the red book."

This was also going to make it more difficult for Eric to function in a sheltered workshop environment, where many tasks are color-coded on purpose, so clients are not required to have a high level of reading. It would still be possible for him to succeed there, but he would have to be taught ways to compensate. "Compensate" was going to be an important skill for Eric the rest of his life.

I guess that is my lesson from Eric. In my early years of teaching, I thought about just teaching kids everything I could. That's not completely wrong, but it's not always possible. I had to accept that I was not going to be able to teach Eric his colors. I had to teach him how to make up for, or how to live successfully with, not being able to see colors.

Being able to compensate for lack of something is an important skill for everyone. If you can't do triple-digit decimal division in your head like my husband does, you adapt by getting out the calculator. I have girls in my class right now who have no father in their lives. How do they compensate for that? Well, there are good ways and not-so-good ways. We try to teach kids positive ways to compensate. We try to teach about balance in their lives. So many things missing; and how to make up for them all? It's what gets me up every morning.

14   ALWAYS IN A HAPPY PLACE

She did not like being called "Little Jody". When she heard that name, she would stop right where she was, roll up her shirt sleeves, and show you her tiny biceps.

Then Jody might shake her fist at you and say, "I'm not little! I could beat you up!" She always said it with a grin in her voice. Jody was a happy kid. She was fifteen and about 4'8" tall. That was as tall as she was going to get.

Jody was intellectually challenged and looked like a little pixie....oops, like a pixie...leave off the part about being little, please. She had brown eyes that always were darting around, looking for something to do. Jody was able to read sight words, and was beginning to read with some basic phonics. She could tell time and count money. She was extremely proud of the Plexiglas windshield scraper she made in shop class.

She was very slender and moved quickly. She loved to run, swing on the playground, and climb on the jungle gym. Jody was a tomboy, for sure, and she always would be. "Womanhood", as most of us know it, was not in her future.

Jody's medical diagnosis was Turner syndrome. It is one of those rare genetic conditions that special education teachers learn about throughout their careers. They don't teach it in the college classes; you just learn as you go.

Turner syndrome is a rare chromosomal disorder that affects only females (1 in 2500), and only 8-10% of those affected females are intellectually challenged. The symptoms of girls with this syndrome are short stature, abnormally loose skin on the neck, unusual eyes, a lowered placement of ears, a very small lower jaw, plus they often have heart and kidney problems. Girls with this condition have broad, shield-like chests and elbow deformities that make their arms hang awkwardly.

The underlying cause of Turner syndrome is not known; it does not run in families, and it occurs in a random manner. In all cases, however, there is a partial or complete loss of one of the X (sex) chromosomes. Turner syndrome can cause hyperactivity, gross and fine motor abnormalities, and language delays in those with normal intelligence. Jody had all these symptoms, besides her mental deficiency.

Jody would remain extremely short, never develop breasts or mature sexually, and she would be infertile, due to ovarian failure. Basically, she would always be a little girl. It is like the "Peter Pan" syndrome, only for girls. However, there is nothing cute or romantic about Turner syndrome. Jody had a bad heart. She had folds of skin on the sides of her neck that made her look different enough to be teased in her neighborhood. Her lower jaw deformity made it difficult for her to chew. She was restricted to soft foods, as there was concern she might choke on improperly chewed food. She grew up with those restrictions, so she didn't yearn for caramel apples or popcorn balls at Halloween. She loved Milky Way bars. She didn't drool over a juicy cheeseburger. She loved sloppy joes. Jody was one of those people who made the best of everything.

Despite all her medical problems and mental obstacles, she was a naturally joyful person. She was one of my students who simply was not intelligent enough to know she was not intelligent. That was probably a blessing for her. Without any hormonal development, Jody did not have any attraction to boys. It was not in her chemical make-up; there was no future male/female drama in her life. She had two caring parents and a couple of siblings; she spoke lovingly about them. She appreciated all the friends she had at school. In her world, Jody had no worries. She was always in a happy place! Wouldn't that be a wonderful place to live?

For Jody, that was her reality. In the rest of the world, as we all know, life is not that simple. Take the fifteen-year-old girls who are in my class at this moment, for example. Wow, they would all be light years ahead on the happiness scale if they did not feel attracted to boys! Regularly and unfortunately, their happiness depends on other people, boys in particular. I endeavor daily to help them find contentment and satisfaction within themselves, but it is a monumental uphill battle. They have trouble focusing on anything but boys. Wait, you say, that's normal for teenage girls! Sure it is, but in the meantime, it causes these particularly mentally-unbalanced girls even more angst than normal. I have a job for life.

In reflecting on the reality of our own adult existence, I would be remiss not to mention your bills, your car in need of repairs, your illness, your aged parents, your rebellious teen, your failed diet/exercise program, and your general stress about almost everything. Feel better?

So, as you think about Jody's multiple permanent limitations and her contentment as I have described it, I have a few questions for you. What is the root of your happiness? Are you happy with what you have? Do you know where your joy comes from? Are you afraid of losing it? Are you still searching for contentment? Does it come and go, depending on your mood? Does your bliss depend upon someone else? Just some things to consider.

So now to get to the lesson I learned from Jody. For me, Jody confirmed the belief that a person is about as happy as they make up their mind to be. Half empty/half full. According to Jody's limited but naively wise perspective, the glass was half full of water and half full of air....so it was FULL. My own perception of her permanently pleasant demeanor remains, in my memory, as the perfect example of someone making lemonade out of lemons. Her paradigm was always from a viewpoint of natural positivity. She had not taken a Dale Carnegie class or listened to any inspirational speakers. She was naturally happy. Yeah, that's it....I'm sticking with that....and that's my story. I'm going to be happy. All things considered, I really have nothing to complain about. Because I said so, and Jody showed me how.

FOOTNOTE of interest for all you NCIS Los Angeles fans.

Linda Hunt: A Celebrity with Turner's Syndrome

Linda Hunt was born on April 2, 1945 in Morristown,

New Jersey by the name of Lydia Susanna Hunter. She began her career at a young age as an actor and singer because her mother was a music teacher. She debuted in Hollywood in the 1980's film version of Popeye as Mrs. Oxheart. She is currently known for her role as Hetty Lange on NCIS: Los Angeles. She has also stared in movies such as Pocahontas as Grandmother Willow, Mrs. Munion in Yours, Mine, and Ours, and Shadout Mapes in Dune. Throughout her career, she has won thirteen different awards, such as the 2012 Teen Choice Award for her character on NCIS: Los Angeles and an Oscar for Best Actress in a Supporting Role in 1984 for her movie The Year of Living Dangerously. She has happily lived with her partner, Karen Klein, since 1987. Not only is Linda Hunt an actress, but she also has Turner's Syndrome.

Hunt's condition has caused her to grow to be only four feet and nine inches tall. Despite living with Turner's syndrome, Hunt has grown to be a well-known celebrity. She did not let her condition inhibit her career as an actress. She is considered an inspiration for women with Turner's syndrome that aspire to achieve their goals in life.

15   ROBERT ATE HIS ZIPPER AGAIN

Kids do strange things. We adults laugh, make videos, and sent cute emails all the time about a myriad of weird situations children get themselves into. However, sometimes kids do things that are not funny. I have a picture of Robert scorched into my memory. It's not funny. It is heart-wrenching and haunting. Out of all the students I had in my classes, Robert is probably the one whom it hurts the most to remember. I taught there for nearly ten years and his is probably the face I can picture most clearly. Too clearly.

Robert was average height for a teenager, very thin, and had a shock of short blond hair that stood on end. With one hand, he ran his long bony fingers through his hair constantly, from all directions, so it tilted at different directions on a minute-by-minute schedule. Neither his hands nor his hair were ever very clean, except on the days we went swimming. It's painful to remember how he looked in his swim suit; like a skeleton. The reason Robert was so thin was related to his hyperactivity. He was in constant motion. His hands, his feet; even his shoulders were always moving. He must have burned a million calories per day. His movement was a bit unusual, though, because he wasn't one of those hyperactive students who race around the room. He pretty much stood still and moved. That is, he stayed in one spot, but his body was moving all the time.

By far, the most compelling part of his movement was the way his wild, bright blue eyes constantly swerved back and forth, racing from one person or one object to another. His wild-eyed contact with us was maintained only for a micro-second, and then his eyes would dart to the floor for another micro-second. Robert had most likely been on the receiving end of some physical punishment. I think this is why he stood in one spot instead of bouncing around the room like many hyperactive kids would do. He was trying to be unobtrusive; straining to physically "stay below the radar" of any adult who might be annoyed by him and his perpetual motion.

Robert's most unusual manifestation of his over-activity was chewing on his clothes. Yes, chewing on his clothes, while he was wearing them. About twice every month, I had to rummage through the social worker's closet of extra clothes, and get Robert another jacket. We had three recess periods per day, and we were in a cool climate state. During the school year in that northern clime, from September to May, it is not usually very warm, and kids would need to wear a coat or jacket outside at recess.

Zipped or not, Robert would begin at the top and literally chew the zipper right out of the front of his coat. He would start on the upper right side, pulling it in between his teeth, gnawing at the stitching until he worked the top loose. Working his way down the right side, all the way to the bottom, he would furtively glance around to see if everything going on around him was safe, and then he would gnaw some more. His feet would be moving, one hand would be going through his hair, and the other hand was stuffing his jacket into his mouth while he chewed,

chewed, and chewed.

It usually took him a week or ten days' worth of recesses to decimate the zipper. Then we would get another jacket for him. Why keep giving him another coat when we knew what he was going to do to it? Why not give him something else to chew on? Feed the kid, for crying out loud, if he is so skinny! Can't you teach him not to do that? Wasn't it wrecking his teeth?

Of course, we worked hard with our behavior modification specialists to teach him not to do that. Fail. We gave him plenty to eat......there seemed to be no acceptable substitute for the satisfaction he got from removing those zippers with his teeth. He absolutely would not tolerate a pullover hoodie being put on over his head. He was always so remorseful once his newest jacket was zipperless; he was always sincerely disappointed. Fortunately, his chewing was pretty much on the threads and fabric of his outerwear, so his teeth were fine.

This was complicated by Robert's lower intellectual capacity. His disability was severe. He could not help himself, and try as we might, we could not help him either. Everyone loved him. He harmed no one with his coat chewing. Robert was one of our most even-tempered students; he was cooperative in class. He waited his turn in lunch line; his peers liked him. His idiosyncrasy was distracting, but manageable, as long as the coat donations kept coming in.

I'm not even going to try to describe what happened when someone came up with the idea of putting him into a "snowmobile suit" for recess. As long as you know that those garments have a zipper that runs from the neck nearly all the way down to the knee, I will let you imagine how Robert dealt with that!

Regardless of this interesting habit, Robert did everything else in pretty much the same fashion as all our other students. Sure, that one behavior was quirky, but it made interesting conversation. It became a challenge that we would present to new staff, as they joined us, to see if there were any new ideas for helping him. Regrettably, when he turned twenty-one, we helped him transfer to the group home/sheltered workshop program without solving this puzzle. He would be nearly fifty years old by now, and perhaps he is still chewing the zippers out of his coats.

Robert reminds me of other people that I know now....no, they don't gnaw their zippers....but they have quirky habits that usually harm no one but themselves. If I start listing examples, you will not take the time to think of your own, so I'm not going to give you any clues. You know these people; perhaps you are even one of them. You (or your friend or family member) do something odd, for some known or unknown reason, but it's dramatically different than the rest of the planet. Perhaps it has become a joke to tell at parties, or a family story, or a giggle at the water cooler in the office. It's just crazy...why would they do it like that? Or maybe it is something that they DON'T do, that most of the rest of us do.

If you take time to think about these people you each know...does that really make them all that much different than the rest of us...or that different from Robert? He had lots of "different" things about him, but he was really more LIKE most kids, than unlike them. This is a real truth. "Special" kids are really just kids. No matter what they chew on. Now, quit thinking about all those odd people you know; appreciate everyone for how special they are.

16   MUSCLES UPON MUSCLES

Steven was non-verbal. The year was 1976 and he was seventeen. He had come out of a state institution for the "mentally retarded" in 1975. In 1975 there was a federal law passed, called PL94-142. It protected the right of individuals like Steven to have a free, public education. This public law emptied out many large impersonal warehouse-like state institutions full of intellectually-challenged children, and created countless numbers of group homes where those children could have a more "normal" life. This happened all over the United States. Another student I have written about in my "Overalls and Wonder Bread" chapter, Jeff, also came out of an institution.

Steven was not in my classroom. He was in a room on the first floor, where Miss Harriet was the teacher. Her class was the six lowest-functioning students at our special school. She had four classroom assistants. That made five adults helping six children. Several of her students were wheelchair-bound. None of them were toilet trained. Their IQs were way below 50. They needed a lot of help, believe me.

So, I would walk past Miss Harriet's classroom and see Steven several times every day, as I took my class to gym, to lunch, to the playground, or to shop class or the home economics room.

Steven was not toilet trained, did not use eating utensils, and sat on the floor. He didn't like chairs. He barely tolerated clothing. No shoes, please. Strangely, although Steven spent most of his days sitting nearly motionless on the floor, this very dark-skinned African American young man was almost always glistening with sweat.

When walking past Steven, you absolutely had to look at him. He had the physique of a champion bodybuilder, but he spent most of his days, for most of his life, just sitting. Sitting on the floor. That is not much of a fitness program. Was he pumping iron at home every night?

No..... but Stephen did have his own special way of building muscle. *Isometrics.*

Flexing his muscles, over and over and over and over. I'm quite sure he acquired the habit at a very early age, and was, I'm certain, too low intellectually to even know what he was doing. I don't know how or why he would have started, but while researching this style of muscle building, I have discovered a wide variety of opinions about it. The problem is that there are no studies about a person doing isometrics, every waking hour, for *years and years.*

All I know for sure is that Stephen's days were filled with thousands of muscle contractions. Stephen's movements were pretty much imperceptible, but his results were obvious. After all when you do anything enough times, something happens.

I am reminded of other such repetitive and subtle actions that have created dramatic results. For example:

I wonder how many times a young person heard their mother promise to stop using drugs, before their trust in adults was totally decimated.

I wonder how many times a child has to hear, "You're stupid." before they just quit doing homework and abandon trying to be a good student?

I wonder how many times a young person hears, "You need to get a real job", before they give up on their entrepreneurial or artistic dream?

On the other side of the coin, does it really take that much effort to encourage a young person? "You can do it." Those four simple words, or variations of them, can make a phenomenal difference in the attitude and success of an aspiring, or struggling, young person.

My own father's version of those words was always, "Go get 'em, Tiger!" So I did. After all, I had the full faith and backing of Dad and Mom. That's all it took. Sure, I had encouraging and inspiring teachers who reinforced my parents' biased urgings. I even got a fan letter after a great basketball game from one of my father's business associates, so I knew Dad was bragging about me. It was a little embarrassing, but down deep, it felt good. It kept me pushing myself to be better.

So, what does this have to do with Stephen's bulging biceps? Everything! If you are going to do something over and over and over again, try to make sure it has a positive end purpose. Stephen couldn't help himself. You can!

I could give all kinds of examples, but you know exactly what I am saying. For teachers, and parents especially, the repetition of positives is essential. The more the better. The students need encouragement; just not the fake kind. They need to do something, or at least to try to do something to earn it. And eliminate the put-downs, and the sarcasm. To paraphrase a Jack Nicholson character, "Sarcasm is anger's ugly stepsister."

The potential strength of Stephen remained untested. Who knows what he could have done with his strength? His lower intellectual capacity prevented him from ever being able to use it. However, there are students in classrooms and children in their homes every day who have plenty of potential and intellectual capacity, and they are not being encouraged. If these kids are going to be productive citizens and happy self-supporting people, they need to practice repetitive success!

Flex those muscles! They might be poetry muscles, math muscles, public speaking muscles, science muscles...it doesn't matter...flex them! Smile at these kids, say "Good job!", pat them on the back, put a sticker on their shirt, call their parent and praise them, put their work on display in the hall or classroom.

Beyond this, teach those kids how to praise themselves! When I left for college at age seventeen, my father wasn't right next to me anymore. There was no one saying, "Way to go, Tiger!", so I started talking to myself. "Good job, Terri!", "I can do this!" It worked. I still do it. I motivate myself. Children need to learn to do this. Over and over and over and over.....

17   DEAR OL' SOL

Her name was Solveig (pronounced: Soul' vig). She was very much one of those intrepid northern state "Scandahoovians". I'm really not sure if she was Norwegian, Swedish, or Danish...there were plenty of all three in town; but I know she was old. She was a lead social worker at the special school where I worked. Both of the other social workers were somewhere in their 30s and 40s....but Solveig was ancient compared to them. Ancient, as in stoop-shouldered, skinny legs, old-fashioned dresses, and holding onto the stair railing on the way down the stairs. She said she had never smoked, and I certainly believed her, because she never drank the hard stuff, either, when we had staff parties. Knowing that, I always marveled at how many wrinkles she had....she seemed to have too many for a woman who had obviously engaged in the art of "good, clean living". In hindsight, I suppose Solveig's fair Scandahoovian skin was responsible; it was just too delicate for that blazing hot northern climate week of summer every year..

In Solveig's favor, she had arresting, sparkling blue eyes. Her hair was a pale shade of gray, with natural streaks of pure white. I wish my own hair was going gray in that beautiful way. Solvieg's smile was radiant. She was the first indefatiguably cheerful and perennially positive person I ever met. Solvieg (Sol, as we called her), was a veritable whirlwind of social work at its finest.

There were many fine teachers in our school. Most were young like I was, being closer to twenty-five than thirty-five. We partied at Sunny's pub, twice a month after school, on Friday payday. We told our intellectually disabled kids we were going out for "milk and cookies". Sol never came with us, but she always peeked into our classrooms at the end of those days and told us to have fun and drive safely. She basically functioned as our faculty "mom", in addition to her primary role as a strong advocate for our students and their families. Sol was a persistent detective at ferreting out resources to meet any need that the children or their parents had. I used to tease her about how it seemed she never went home, asking her where the Murphy bed was hidden in her office wall.

Anyway, what has prompted me to write this about Solveig, instead of a student, was a Google search I did. Just out of curiosity, I typed in a few staff names. Up popped a link to Solveig. It was from the school district's employees "recently deceased" list. Coincidentally, and sadly, she passed away exactly one year ago today, March 31, 2012, at the age of ninety-seven. My mind started spinning the numbers....that meant that she was sixty-four years old when I left teaching to be a stay-at-home mom, after the birth of our son Van. We moved to Iowa shortly after that. Whoa...the last time I saw Solveig, she was exactly the same age as I am now. Wait! I was so young then, and as I might have mentioned earlier, she appeared to be so ancient!

I started thinking, 'Is this how my twenty and thirty-something peers at school view me now?' Could I appear to be ancient to them? Sure, I forget some stuff now and then, but I make more fun of myself than any of them do about that. I've had three joints replaced, so I don't need to use the stair railing. My hair isn't gray (Thanks, Faith at Hair To Stay in Johnston). My clothes are pretty standard-issue 'teacher style'. Holiday socks for Christmas and Halloween, comfortable but fashionable shoes, the obligatory sweaters from the Von Maur department store...I confess to owning them all. I don't think they're dowdy.

I feel respected and completely valued by my co-workers, as I felt towards Sol. Never once did I give her any hint that she appeared elderly to me and never spoke about it to anyone else. I did not make fun of her age, doubt her dedication and skill in her field, or mention to her that it might be time to retire. I wasn't raised like that. I was instructed to respect my elders and I did. Yikes, now I am almost an elder myself!

No, I'm NOT! Solveig wasn't old either! After all, my sister Sharon was teaching at Iowa State University in her seventies. I work in Des Moines with a seventy-eight year old teacher. At church, there is an extraordinary woman, also in her seventies, Jane, who is also actively teaching. All three of them have amazing energy levels and love teaching. I know that I will not be teaching when I am in my seventies, but I salute those who do.

I especially salute Solveig, who worked with the same challenging students I have been writing about, but she was more than twice my age at the time. Any kid can drain a teacher, but special kids are particularly good at it. She may have been ancient, but I don't remember ever seeing her look tired. Solveig always looked like she had just finished a great nap, with her bright blue eyes and engaging smile. Any looming crisis or pressing need brought to her attention was immediately transformed into an opportunity to be creative and compassionate.

You have been gone a couple of years now, and you surely earned your rest, dear ol' Sol. I'm trying to remember how you operated when you were my age. My steps might be more spry and my wardrobe may be a little bit less dowdy, but as I strive daily to match your charm and effectiveness, I fall short. I can't promise anything, Sol, but I will truly give each day a good ol' Scandahoovian try. Thank you for your shining example.

18   LOOKING PAST THE SCARS

Jeffrey looked a bit like Mel Gibson in the movie, <u>The Man Without A Face</u>, only worse. I looked online for images of burned faces and I found some that were less scarred than Mel and some were more scarred....more like the face of my former student Jeffrey. Jeffrey's facial features were barely recognizable, and his whole head was scarred; he could not grow hair on his head. He was a teenage boy wearing a terrible wig. There was one image I found online that looked very much like him, a wig perched on top of the scarred skull, but it did not at all represent the real Jeffrey. His "inside" was what was really exceptional and is what made it possible to look past the scars.

Jeffrey was a physician's son. When he was four years old, there was a fire in their house. A frightened little Jeffrey hid under his bed, was difficult to find, and although he survived, he was grotesquely scarred for life...on the outside.

On the inside, he was the "Jeff" in my earlier chapter about Wendy, <u>I'm Going to Marry Jeff, & We're Going to Get a Poodle</u>. Wendy, as I wrote and I hope you have already read, did not live long enough to marry Jeffrey, but he was definitely the marrying kind. He was wonderful kid who had a seriously life-changing bad break. His intellectual functioning had been normal for a four-year-old before the fire, but that changed drastically. There seemed to be no definitive explanation; it could have been post-traumatic stress or perhaps brain damage due to lack of oxygen to his brain during the fire. His diminished intellectual capacity could have been a combination of factors, but whatever the cause, Jeffrey was in my special class in our special school.

Many of the students in my class did not look "normal", for a variety of reasons. Kids like Scott, in the chapter <u>Silence Is Not Always Golden,</u> or Troy in <u>Wanna See My Fried Egg Face?</u> are two examples. Scott looked average, but his disability caused him to present himself in an out-of-ordinary manner. Troy was a student with Down syndrome, so he appeared physically different. Well, Jeffrey didn't look intellectually challenged, just horribly disfigured....on the outside.

However, the inside of Jeff was charming, kind, and very gentlemanly. He took school seriously, but he knew how to have fun. His scarred limbs somewhat inhibited his full physical inclusion in Special Olympic athletics and regular playground activities, but he always made a sporting effort to participate as much as he could. He was curious and had a tremendous work ethic. He took much pride in achieving all his IEP (Individualized Educational Plan) goals. He loved working in the woodshop as much as his beloved Wendy did.

My most indelible memory of Jeffrey is from one of the weekly trips that a fellow teacher and I took to the local Farmer's Market. This market held daily, Monday through Saturday. We would leave pretty early on Friday mornings and walk our students nearly a half of a mile from our downtown school to the market on the near north side of town. Farmers would back their trucks up to the long, raised cement slabs and put out boxes of their fresh produce. It was always a busy place, and in the fall, there were almost always several elementary school groups there for a field trip.

One fine fall day, we got to the market and there was only one shiny yellow school bus there. The children getting off the bus appeared to be kindergartners...also fresh and shiny, very new to school, and probably on their first field trip. They seemed a bit unruly, compared to our experienced and well-trained adolescents.

As the little students lined up in their field trip "buddy pairs", I noticed a couple of them were pointing at Jeffrey. They weren't laughing, just pointing, and actually looking a bit frightened. Jeffrey's looks could have that effect, especially on young children. On our other trips to the market, it was not unusual for students to stare, but that day it was more serious than staring. Jeffrey also noticed them eyeing him.

He made a U-turn and walked right up to them. Their teacher was at the bus door, and suddenly realized that she was farther away from her students than she wanted to be. I quickly followed Jeff, not knowing what his reaction might be. He had never been confrontational before. The two children took a step back, and Jeffrey stopped in front of where they had been standing. By now, many of the other "buddy pairs" were observing him.

What came out of Jeffrey was amazing.

In a strong and clear voice he said to the children, "It's OK to stare at me. I look awful, but I can't help it. When I was little like you, my house caught on fire. I hid under the bed. If you are ever in a fire, make sure you get out. Get out fast. Don't hide under your bed."

One of the pointers asked, "Does it hurt?"

"No, not anymore, now it just looks bad."

"I'm sorry."

"It's OK, just don't hide if your house catches fire. Get out. Bye." Jeffrey turned and walked away, to catch up with our group.

By this time, the kindergarten teacher had arrived. She just looked at me as I stood there. Jeffrey was gone.

Kindergarten teacher asked, "Was there a problem?"

"No problem", I proudly replied. "Jeffrey just gave some of your students an important lesson in fire safety. They can tell you about it."

Kindergarten teacher said, "I don't know what to say."

I answered, "Just promise me you'll make sure they remember this."

Kindergarten teacher, "I promise. Thank you."

I always took my two oldest children, Jenipher and Charles, to school during the school year, for occasions such as field days, open houses, and Special Olympic activities. They were exposed to those two hundred intellectually-challenged kids from the time they were about five and six years old, until we moved back to Iowa when they were twelve and thirteen. Jenny and Charlie played with them, talked to them, and spent time getting to know them. It didn't matter that they looked different, or spoke funny, or sometimes did strange things. I taught my children that those students were so much more LIKE them, than they were UNLIKE them.

What was important was what those students were like on the inside. They were adored by their parents, just like Jenny and Charlie were. They liked to tease and be teased. They laughed at jokes, and played jokes. These kids liked hugs, just like Jenny and Charlie. They were sad when their pet fish died. They liked to learn, and they liked to tell what they learned. That is exactly what Jeffrey did. He may have appeared to be the "r" word, but he had a very important lesson to share. And he did it very well.

When I reported the farmers market incident to Jeffrey's parents, they were justifiably impressed. They already knew they had a very special kid; what Jeffrey looked like on the outside was gruesome to some, but not at all to them. What Jeffrey looked like on the inside was beautiful to everyone who took the time to get past the scars and get to know him.

That's all that really matters...with anyone. Our "scars" might not be as obvious as Jeffrey's were, but we all have them. And we have lessons to give others, if they take the time to get to know us.

I'm so glad I had time to get to know Jeffrey.

19   LEAD, NOT DIAMONDS, ON THE SOLES OF HER SHOES

Remember those ridiculous inflatable punching clowns you bought for your kids when they were young? They were so much fun because they never stayed down! That goofy red-lipped clown would bounce right back up in your face, ready for the next punch! Hold that image in your mind while I tell you about Bonnie.

Bonnie was a student in my classroom. She was born with cerebral palsy and was also intellectually challenged. She was a tall and very slim wisp of a girl. When she wore green, she resembled a blade of grass...that's how thin she was. And the height, from my point of view, is always an advantage. At 5 feet 9 inches, I always tell people I would rather be taller than shorter.

For Bonnie, her height was a distinct disadvantage. It made her beanpole-like frame even more unstable than it normally would have been. Her muscular control, because of her condition, gave Bonnie a wobbly and teetering gait. She had been unable to walk without tipping over until she was about five years old. Her wise parents decided to try a technique that would keep her out of a wheelchair for the rest of her life; they put lead weights on the bottom of her shoes.

As you know, lead is extremely heavy. One cubic inch weighs over one-third of a pound. So, a piece of lead about the size of a standard dry-erase marker would weigh a pound. That's a hefty marker! Now, imagine having someone put about four pounds of lead on the bottom of each of your shoes. It would surely slow you down, but it would also be terribly difficult to tip you over!

Picture this tall, very thin girl, taking slow steps with heavy weights on the bottom of her shoes. She still rocked side to side, appearing as though she might tip over, but she never did. The way Bonnie was able to drag her iron-soled saddle shoes across the floor made it seem as though the floor was magnetized. Gravity was her friend as she lurched forward. Bonnie never complained, even though each step was obviously a monumental struggle. She was upright and independently mobile; mission accomplished. To paraphrase Paul Simon's song:

> She's got lead on the soles of her shoes.
> Well, that's one way to lose
> These walking blues.
> Lead on the soles of your shoes.

Problem solved! The End? Not quite.

The heaviness of Bonnie's shoes make me think of the weight of whatever it is that holds each of us in our "place"; our "anchor", so to speak. What keeps us from toppling over and crashing to the floor? I like to think I'm "grounded", but when I really pause for a moment, I start to consider the possibilities. Am I? It feels like it.

Seldom, if ever, do I get that overwhelmed feeling that used to come when I was younger. When I thought I had to say "yes" to everyone else. When I thought I had to do everything by myself and when it all had to be done perfectly. Oh yeah...that kind of thinking is not an anchor....it's more like a ball and chain. Now, I have become more like that silly clown who never stays down.

What grounds me now is simple....a family I adore, a job I love, and knowing I am a child of God.

It's just that basic. Although your "lead" may be something completely different than mine, usually simpler is better.

Almost as easy as putting lead on the bottom of a teetering young lady's shoes. Who knew? What anchors you?

20   CHOCOLATE MILK AND
BURNING GARAGES

"No legacy is so rich as honesty."
- William Shakespeare

Dale appeared to be the freckle-faced red-haired boy that my mother always said she wanted when she had a son. That didn't happen; she got me, a blonde, blue-eyed girl. I told her about Dale once, and she confirmed for me that she was glad she didn't give birth to him. Together, we prayed for Dale's mother.

Reflecting on this young man, I have recently decided that the school year I spent working with Dale was the equivalent of an extra year of a college education. He helped me prepare for so many of the students who followed him into my classroom in the future. Many people who are not in education assume that all intellectually challenged students are pretty much the same. They assume that these kids are not as smart as other kids, so even though they may be "more work" in the classroom, they probably are not as complicated as your average teenager. FALSE!

Dale was one of the most complicated students I have

ever had. He appeared to be an average sixteen year old. He wore braces, walked fast, talked fast, and ate like a pig. He wasn't overweight, but still had a thin layer of 'cush' on his body and face. His round impish face was often red and flushed, like he had just run a mile, or was terribly embarrassed. He dressed quite neatly, usually in jeans and the plaid shirts that were so popular in the mid-1970s.

Where do I start? He fidgeted with his hands incessantly. They were always moving, as were his eyes. Dale looked like he thought he was being watched every minute, and he wanted to see who was watching him. He behaved as though he was afraid of being accused of something....and he looked guilty all the time. When something suspicious would happen in my room, I often wondered if it could be Dale, but I never was able to pin anything on him. He always denied it and usually had a good story to back up his pleas of innocence.

The first time I actually caught him doing something is a moment I will never forget. I can picture it in my mind like it happened yesterday, not thirty years ago.

Our school cooks kept all the cartons of milk for the students in a large cooler, in a small room off the kitchen. This room had a door going into the kitchen, and another door going into the school gymnasium/cafeteria. The cooks were in the kitchen all day, from the time school started until about an hour before the students went home. They had been noticing some of the cartons of chocolate milk were missing, and figured out that the only time someone could be stealing the milk was in the hour between the time the cooks left and the time the school buses came to pick up the students. We lined up all the students in the gym to wait for their buses every afternoon, and somehow one (or more) of them was sneaking into that room and getting into the cooler to take the milk.

That should not have been hard to stop. But it was. Dale was clever.

Dale would line up for his bus with other kids from his side of Minneapolis. He would slip out of line by asking to use the restroom. The restroom door was just around the corner from the cafeteria, so he would be allowed to go on his own. Apparently, he never actually went to the restroom. He would go out the door to the hallway, run down the hall and come back in the door at the other end of the cafeteria. He would pinch or hit one of the non-verbal students, lined up waiting for their bus, at that end of the cafeteria, and they would begin to yell. Dale would then duck out into the hall again, race down to the kitchen door, and cut through there into the room with the milk cooler in it. He would gulp down a couple of cartons of chocolate milk, and then come out to line up for his bus again. With the staff distracted by the pinched student at the other end of the cafeteria, Dale could get back in his bus line without being seen. Quite a devious plan.

I only figured this out because I had stepped out the back door of the cafeteria to look for the buses one day, so I missed the commotion Dale created at the far end of the cafeteria. When I walked back into the school, I observed Dale in the milk room, with chocolate milk dripping out of both corners of his mouth. Confronting him was one of the most disturbing and surreal events in my career. I think it is in a three-way tie with The Salad Meltdown Lesson and Rosemary's Shower.

"Dale, what's in the hand behind your back?"

"Nuthin'"

"Dale, please show me what's in your hand."

He showed me the empty chocolate milk carton. He insisted he did not take it. He insisted he did not drink it. When I asked him about the milk dripping down his face, he used his sleeve to make it disappear, and kept insisting he did not take or drink any chocolate milk.

Yes, I had caught him, practically in the act. There was no reasonable explanation for how the carton got in his hand and how the milk came to be dripping down his face, except the observable fact that he stole the milk and drank it. Yet, he denied it.

"I didn't do anything," he said. He put the carton down on the cooler and walked out to his place in the school bus line.

"Dale, I saw the carton. You had milk in your mouth. You took the milk."

"I didn't do anything."

What kind of circumstances or life experiences lead up to such an exchange? The term 'pathological liar' popped into my head. Actually, that term can be interchanged with 'compulsive liar' and 'habitual liar'.

This condition has been defined as "falsification entirely disproportionate to any discernible end in view, may be extensive and complicated, and happen over a period of years, or perhaps a whole lifetime."

Dale may have been aware he was lying, or he may have believed he was telling the truth. Not a lot of research has been done, but one study estimates a rate of one in 1,000 juvenile offenders. Dale did not have a criminal juvenile history.....yet. The average age of onset for this kind of chronic lying is sixteen years. Forty percent of cases also involved some central nervous system abnormality, and Dale's intellectual disability would fall into that category.

It is a mental illness. Uncommon, difficult to explain, and most likely it was going to create lifelong problems for Dale. We would just have to watch him carefully. Very carefully. The social worker agreed, and Dale was escorted everywhere he went in the building.

Then the fires started.

They were always early in the morning, always a garage, and in Dale's neighborhood. The police, the fire department, and the neighbors were stymied.

Then one day, after about eight garage fires in a three week period, Dale came into my classroom, with a distinct odor of gasoline on his clothes. He said he was helping his dad at the gas pump and over-filled the tank; some gasoline had splashed out onto his pants. I knew he was lying about it, because he lived with his mother. His father didn't even live in-state.

It just made me sick. I had a horrible feeling that Dale was involved in the fires. They were so dangerous. A flaming garage could set a house on fire. Eventually, someone was going to get hurt.

I took Dale down to the social worker's office. I explained to her what I thought was going on. She called the police and she called Dale's mother. Officers came to talk to Dale. They took him home, spoke with his mother, and searched Dale's house and garage. They found evidence in Dale's bedroom and outside his window that indicated Dale had been crawling in and out of the window. Dale's mother confessed that she had seen him sneaking back in the window on two mornings when there had been garage fires. Dale was arrested. Of course, he completely denied everything, and he had elaborate stories to explain it all.

His mother's testimony, along with the evidence from the house and the garage, convicted Dale. He was tried in juvenile court, not as an adult, because of his severe mental disability. His mother agreed to have him sent to a state mental institution. Dale was going to be held there, at least until he was twenty-five, or until it could be declared that he was no longer a danger. He was sent to a place where he was going to be able to get some help that he desperately needed.

I have wondered for many years about Dale. His bold, blatant lies still haunt me. We have probably all been told lies, to our face, that we immediately know are not true at all. It is frustrating, but we deal with it by ferreting out the truth and shining the light on it. Still, even with the truth exposed, it hurts our hearts that someone would try to deceive us. With Dale's 'condition' it seems like he was not really capable of telling the truth. It doesn't sound right to me, but Dale couldn't help but tell lies. Some of his lies were to keep himself out of trouble. Some of his lies were to make himself seem more grand than he really was. Dale told some lies because he opened his mouth and out came anything but the truth. On top of all that, he was a pyromaniac.

Could he have told the truth if he had wanted to? Why keep lying if there is nothing to be gained by it? How frustrating is it to hear a lie that you know is a lie, and you also know that the person lying will get absolutely no benefit from lying to you? Are they lying just to lie? Just to get one over on you?

If the only answer was, "It's a mental illness. There is no understanding it," then it was even worse. In my mind, it was like having a doctor's note for lying. "Please excuse Dale. He has a good reason for lying and you cannot hold him responsible. Oh, and he sets fires, too. Can't help that either." What?

OK, I can deal with the mental illness part...I am older now. It seemed like a lame explanation for despicable behavior when I was younger. Lying was already one of my pet peeves, and then I met Dale, who basically had a doctor's note to do it. Grrrrr.

Lying was a serious flaw in your personal character....that's how I was raised. Experience has now taught me there are cases like this, and I cannot waste time fussing over them. He couldn't help it. Over the past thirty years, I have had many students with a variety of mental health issues in my classroom. They have enough problems without being blamed for their mental illness. No one chooses it.

However....lying is harmful, no matter what the circumstance. It harms the person who tells the lie and it harms the person who is told the lie. The argument has been made repeatedly for "little white lies" being allowed. Ugh.

A person who will lie about the little things will also lie about the important things.

Honesty in little things is not a little thing.

Just tell the truth.

I REALLY try to impress this on every student I get in my classroom.

This is when I wish everyone was older, like I am. If I were to tell a lie, I would probably forget that I told it, and also forget WHO I told. The trouble would start then. Who did I tell? What did I tell them? What did I tell this other person? Oh my goodness....my memory is just too poor to tell any lies. I couldn't possibly keep them straight.

One of the richest men in Des Moines spoke at a Drake University graduation that I attended. He said the NUMBER ONE RULE in life, is to tell the truth; in your personal life, in your professional life, in all your relationships. Tell the truth.

Try hard. Unless you are one in 1,000, you have no doctor's note.

21 UPSIDE DOWN ON THE TRUNK OF A POLICE CAR

John was another student of mine, who had come out of a state institution. He had a strange last name; a French name. He smiled a lot. His skin was a very yellowish color...he did not look like a healthy fourteen-year-old, but the special group home where he lived assured us it was only due to all the prescription medications John took.

Cognitively, he was quite low-functioning. What he lacked in natural intellect, however, he more than made up for in energy. He was the epitome of perpetual motion. Even when John was medicated, and on his best day, the 1:1 classroom helper assigned to him was constantly on the run. Literally, on the run. John was quick and he was cagey. If something caught his interest, he would find a way to get to it; the fastest way possible. My daughter had been like that, and when she started walking at the age of nine months (running at ten months), I bought a cute little pink canvas harness for her, with a leash on it. I was already expecting our son, so it was the only way I could keep up with her and make sure she was safe. Hindsight tells me that we should have had a harness for John.

One of the best things about teaching in the city was all

the lakes and parks. There was a beautiful lake only a block from our school, but it didn't have the ice cream counter and fishing dock like another local lake did. So, our end-of-the-year picnic, with the class of my teacher-friend Brian, was always at the lake with the fishing dock and treats.

About twenty teenagers with intellectual challenges and pretty close to a dozen staff headed to the picnic in a caravan of school vans. We had fishing poles in the back of one, along with our picnic lunch and some outside game equipment...including the large colorful parachute the kids loved to bounce playground balls on. It was our first public outing with John. Just to be sure we could keep track of him at the lake, it was decided to have Brian and the associate "double-team" John.

Everything was going quite smoothly and as planned. After all, Brian and I were experienced picnic planners; we would play some games, do a little fishing, eat lunch, get ice cream, and then load a bunch of exhausted kids back into the vans.

I was in line with some of my students to get ice cream, when I heard a big splash; then another big splash immediately followed. I turned around, towards the lake, just in time to see John's 1:1 associate flailing in the water on the south side of the dock, and Brian was on the north side of the dock...also in the water. He had pushed them both into the lake! John was running back up the dock, towards the ice cream stand. As he approached, I could tell he was not going to stop; he appeared to be rushing straight past us...toward a busy four-lane Lake Street, a well-traveled thoroughfare going past the north side of the lake.

I grabbed an ice cream cone from a nearby student and

ran after John, thinking I could convince him to stop his escape by offering him a treat. It worked! He heard me hollering. "Ice cream, John! Ice cream!", and screeched to a halt at the entrance to the parking lot. I caught up with him and handed him the drippy cone.

John had just started licking it when he saw Brian and the associate, dripping wet, striding toward us. He started to run again, but I quickly grabbed his shirt. Brian used his most soothing voice to assure John that he was not angry. We really didn't want him to take off again. I transferred my grip from his shirttail to his belt, just to have a little better control. John seemed to settle down and once again he became intent on consuming the ice cream.

We started walking him back to the group. I let go of his belt so he could hold hands with the associate. They were a great match of student/staff and it was a child/parent sort of hand holding. We three adults were talking as the four of us walked; John was closest to the parked cars. I looked over at John, and the ice cream cone was gone. I looked back and did not see it on the ground, so I figured he had wolfed it down. Wrong.

Just as we got back to the curb of the parking lot, we saw a police car back out a space in the lot. John also looked, screamed, "WAIT", and broke free from the handhold of the associate. The officer did not hear him, and proceeded to pull out of the lot and into the street. That was when we saw what had happened to John's ice cream cone...for some reason, John had turned it upside down on the trunk of the police car!

John broke into a record-breaking sprint to retrieve his cone...right down the street! Brian was the fastest of the three of us, so he took off after John. The associate and I ran to get one of the vans, in case Brian was not fast enough to catch John. Luckily, Brian was able to catch up with him and once again gain control by grabbing his belt. Our staff had all been trained in safe ways to restrain students who were in danger of hurting themselves or others, so Brian switched from the belt grasp to a cross-armed type of bear hug from which even a very squirmy John could not escape.

When I pulled up next to them in the van, Brian had been able to lower John onto the sidewalk, and was trying to get him to relax, but John was becoming more and more frantic, screaming loudly for his ice cream and thrashing all over the sidewalk. The associate and I joined Brian in trying to soothe John and quiet him down.

It was just after noon, and the trendy shopping area of town was bustling with folks having lunch in the cozy cafes and sidewalk patios. We were quite a spectacle. After about five minutes, it became apparent that we needed to get John into the van and back to school. He was totally out of control.

Then I remembered the parachute…maybe it was still in the back seat! I retrieved it, with its rainbow of brightly colored panels. We unfolded it as quickly as we could, scooted one edge under John, and rolled him up in it like a taquito. His head stuck out of the end. He was bundled as tightly as a nursery-blanketed newborn and in less than a minute, he went from screeching to calm…then to a smiling serenity.

"Ice cream?" he asked sweetly.

"We're going back to school, John. We'll get ice cream there. You just relax, okay?"

"Okay."

We heard a smattering of applause from the street-side bistro tables. All I could think about was how long it was going to take me to write up the incident report for this fiasco. Brian drove the twenty or so blocks back to school, dropped off the three of us, and then drove back to the lake to help retrieve the rest of the students. The policeman must have been oblivious to what was going on behind him, because he never stopped. I have always wondered what he thought when he found the ice cream mess on his trunk.

So, this "lesson learned" is all about preparation. Two things I always try to have close by: a good team and a big parachute. Not literally of course, but figuratively, for sure. Everyone needs a few other people they can depend on, and they also need a parachute, or a Plan B. Plan A does not always go as planned and sometimes the result takes more than one person to clean up.

Also, if you are lucky, the police don't get involved.

22   LULU DOWN NOW!

LuLu was a real sweetheart. She was a slightly built, seventeen-year-old girl with Down syndrome, who had a most charming and delicate way of gesturing with her hands. Many times when I watched her, she almost looked like a ballerina posing. She mostly used sign language to communicate, but she did have a few simple words and commands to make her needs known.

Whenever we had to go somewhere in the school building, or even outside the building, if LuLu went with us, we always had to allow quite a bit of extra time to get where we were going. Most of the severely intellectually challenged kids we taught moved slowly, except for the hyperactive ones, so we usually crept along....but eventually arrived at our destination.

LuLu made the treks even longer. Serious heart problems plagued her frail body, and she had amazingly developed an automatic compensation strategy. When her body figured out that her heart was not able to pump enough blood to her upper body, she instantly dropped to a squat. I would hear, "LuLu down now!" and know we were all going to stop in our tracks until she felt ready to proceed.

The school nurse explained that this response was most likely LuLu's body recognizing it did not have enough oxygen for her to keep going, and perhaps she even felt a little dizzy. By folding her body up in a squat, LuLu was able to better utilize the limited oxygen, reserving less of it for her lower body and more of it for her upper body and brain. Many times, several of her friends would squat next to her and pat her on the back, their way of showing their support and human compassion. A group of students squatting on the sidewalk always got a few puzzled looks from strangers, if we were on a hike to the park, but it never really bothered us.

It was usually less than five minutes and LuLu was upright and moving forward again. She always had a smile on her sweet, little pale face and never failed to add, "Thanks, all better." Depending on how far we were walking, she might have to squat one or two times, but she always knew when it was time. LuLu knew her limit. She was in touch with her body, or maybe LuLu's body was in touch with her.....either way, when it was time for a break...she took one. She would just drop to the floor. Bam. Squat. "LuLu down now."

LuLu was a genius, really. We should all be as wise, or in tune with ourselves as LuLu was. What if we could automatically know when it was time to quit?

Too much work or stress? Take a break!

Got your energy back? Get busy again!

Too much fun? Had enough to drink? Stop!

Too much to eat? Go for a walk!

Angry...going to explode? Take a break. Say a prayer.

We all need something to aspire to, I suppose. I am going to keep trying to take a lesson from LuLu. I used to over-do a lot of the time. I'd just keep going and keep going, until I was completely exhausted. I'd like to think it's maturity and wisdom that has made me slow down, but it's probably just old age. Either way, "Terri down now."

23   I NOT A QUITTER

.

So, have you ever had a blister on the bottom of your foot? On your heel? On your toes? Ever had blisters on the bottom of your foot, on your heel, AND on your toes, all at the same time?

Well, if you haven't had this misfortune, just imagine it for a moment.....would you try to take all those blisters on a ten mile hike through the woods?

This is about a student we called Rebby. He was in my class of students with intellectual challenges....about 30 years ago, so he would be 45 years old now. Rebby was in the Boy Scout troop at our special school. Rebby had Down syndrome. One of the characteristics of Down syndrome is a gait characterized by foot shuffling/scuffing ...whatever you want to call it. Rebby did not pick up his feet very well when he walked. He got all the way to fifteen years old, and this gait had never caused him many problems...maybe an occasional trip on a sidewalk crack, but nothing serious....until it came to the very exclusive and extremely difficult badge that Rebby made up his mind to earn at Boy Scout camp.

Every summer, I took about a dozen of our special needs Boy Scouts to a massive and quite remote Boy Scout

Camp in the northern part of the state. During the first two week trip up there, we learned a lot about the activities and opportunities available to the scouts. The one that all the boys wanted to do was 'The Trail'. This badge could only be earned by walking TEN miles on their special trail, in one day. Ha! Most of my students usually walked no further than from their house to their special school bus, which was parked right out in front.

That first year, we did not attempt the ten mile hike. We knew we had to talk to parents and doctors first. Rebby was adamant. He wanted that badge. He pestered his parents; he got clearance from his doctor; and he was eager to go back the next summer. We usually went scouting in August, because my students attended a five-day-a-week summer school/day camp in June and July. We decided to use those two months to build up some endurance for our attempt at The Trail. Rebby was pumped!

Sadly, after the first day of summer school, with only a one-half mile practice walk, Rebby had a blister on his heel. The next day, he came with a big smile and a box of band aids in his backpack. We went another half-mile, and Rebby had another blister on the bottom of his big toe. After about two weeks, be had worked our way up to a full two miles, and Rebby had band aids all over his feet. Mom and Dad had purchased some hiking boots along with several pair of thick socks, and those made an enormous difference. It really helped and his blisters slowly healed. He smiled all day long. He brought his water bottle with him every day. He had a bandanna in his back pocket, which he used for all the sweat that dripped from him as we plodded along in the bright sunshine. He just kept smiling. "Gonna earn my badge!" was his mantra, as he dragged those heavy boots farther and farther every day.

By the time we loaded the bus with our twelve Boy Scouts and four staff members, we felt they were ready for The Trail...although I suspected it was going to be more like The Trial. It was about a six hour bus trip, by Greyhound, from the city to a very small town near the camp. Then we took one of those old, rickety scout camp school buses to our campsite. The boys were all tuckered out, so we sorted them out in their tents, prepared a simple meal of hot dogs with 'fixings', gave them their night-time medications, and zipped them into their sleeping bags.

Rebby was the first boy out of his tent in the morning. He was already dressed in his tan Boy Scout uniform. "Gonna earn my badge!" was the first thing out of his mouth. It was difficult, but I had to explain to him that we needed to have one practice day, and then we would take to The Trail on Wednesday. I told him to go put on his hiking boots, which were quite broken in by now, very comfortable, and ready to carry him the required distance.

"No boot in my bag. Think they at home, on bed." Oh dear...no hiking boots for Rebby. How was he going to hike ten miles in his tennis shoes? He had blisters after one-half mile in June!

"Well, we will practice today in your tennis shoes and maybe Mom can send those boots up here tomorrow," was my immediate suggestion.

That did not work out at all. Mom and Dad had left for a vacation, and were already out of town. They would not be able to send the boots. Rebby was going to hike in his tennis shoes....the ones that gave him blisters on long walks.

110

During summer school, we had been walking on sidewalks and bike paths around the lakes, and they were pretty level. I had assumed that the trail at camp would be along the dirt roads that wound through the many acres of northern woods. Nope. Upon arriving at camp, I learned that we were going to be walking ten miles on paths through rugged woods, up pine tree covered inclines, along the slippery banks of the lake, across little creeks, and over rocks. The route had been set up many years ago, and was designed to be challenging.

We had pumped up the kids for this hike during June and July. We had to at least attempt it! The Scoutmaster who was helping us with all our other activities at camp said he planned to send two college-age Eagle Scouts with us on our hike. They would have a first aid kit, extra water, and moleskin with them.

Moleskin? What was moleskin? It sounded creepy to me...but I was relieved to learn that it is a valuable treatment for dealing with blisters. It is sort of like a thick padded band aid, with a hole cut in the middle. It surrounds the blister without covering it, and cushions it from further rubbing. We knew that Rebby would develop blisters and would most likely also refuse to quit until he finished the whole ten miles and earned his badge. Rebby was a pretty stubborn kid. He was otherwise cooperative and very sweet, but once he made up his mind about something, he stuck with it to the very end.

So the day of the hike arrived. We started right after breakfast; about eight o'clock in the morning. Each boy had his lunch in his backpack; we expected to be finished in time for dinner, hopefully by six in the evening. It was going to be a long day. Fortunately, the weather was going to be 70 degrees and overcast, neither heat nor rain were going to be a concern. We estimated it would take ten hours to walk ten miles.

I cannot give you a blow-by-blow, mile-by-mile recollection of our hike. It was a long time ago, but I very plainly remember Rebby's statement as we reached each mile marker, "I not a quitter...I keep walking." Each mile, he repeated it. The Eagle Scouts kept a close eye on him, stopping the group many times to remove Rebby's shoes, and apply more moleskin to newly formed blisters. Both feet, by the time we were done, were plastered with multiple patches of moleskin.

Rebby was limping, but he never quit. Between the two final markers, Mile 9 and Mile 10, Rebby's fellow scouts cheered and sang to Rebby. They chanted and laughed; they were all dirty, exhausted, and sore, but they all marched on...every single one of them finished!

When we got to the ten mile marker, the two Eagle Scouts picked Rebby up, using a four-handed "fireman's carry", and transported him all the way back to his tent. It was about a quarter of a mile from the finish. The camp nurse came and checked Rebby's feet. None of the blisters had broken, thanks to the moleskin.

After dinner, we all gathered around the campfire and the Scoutmaster held a ceremony, presenting each scout with a "The Trail" badge. Rebby cried. I cried. The Eagle Scouts cried. Rebby's friends cheered for him, and for themselves. The Eagle Scouts and I received many hugs from all the boys. Within fifteen minutes after the ceremony, however, all the boys had received their bedtime medications, and they were all asleep on their cots. I needed no medication... I just collapsed on my cot; I think I was asleep before my head hit the pillow.

To this day, the hike on The Trail is on my life's Top Ten Moments list.

To this day, I remember the lesson I learned from Rebby on that trail. Never give up on yourself.

I have always had "Never Give Up On Anyone" printed on my teacher business cards. It's a tag line on my email signature. I have a poster of it hanging in my classroom. Rebby did a little change-up on my motto! He changed "anyone" to "yourself". What is the difference? Doesn't "anyone" include you?

For me, I had always been focused on others; my friends, my family, my students. As the summer experience with Rebby was unfolding, I had been through a divorce, my mother was very ill, and I had a stressful job (even though I loved it, it was very challenging). I was constantly going to the wine bottle in my refrigerator. That part was a little scary, but I was more worried about everyone else.

I don't know exactly how, but going through this experience with Rebby changed my life. I felt more confident. I made mental lists of all the things I was doing right. I discovered I could manage my life and not feel twinges of panic all the time. I was able to relax, without the wine, but when things got tough for a while, I found I mentally braced myself and got strong enough to deal with it all. "I not a quitter" echoed in my brain.

It still does. Thanks, Rebby!

24   THE WORST MOM COMPETITION

Tim's mother filled the doorway of my classroom. "Get in here, stupid! You're in this room every day. Are you getting dumber AND blinder?"

I was about to meet the woman Tim called his 'mean ma'. I could be trite and call her a proverbial 'piece of work', but that would be too kind. She was the absolute worst mother I ever met. In the past twenty-two years, since she first crossed the threshold of my classroom, she has not been topped. I have met drug-addicted mothers, stripper mothers, prostitute mothers, and even two mothers who actually moved out of the state while their child was at school, but Tim's mother gets the prize.

She was just plain mean. I am not going to dignify her by naming her...truly, I have forgotten her name. Any of my readers who know me also know that I pride myself on being able to forget bad things. I have dragged this abomination of a human being out from the depths of my bad memories and shall recreate her here, only to serve as an example of how much damage a bad parent can do to a child.

During this parent/teacher conference when I first

met her, we discussed what the plans were for Tim's transition to adulthood; he was going to be eighteen in a few months. Her contribution to that conversation was simply, "I can't wait until he turns eighteen and I can be rid of him."

So, it was shortly after I met Tim's mother that I started giving my students a standard message when they brought their parents to a school conference with me. I'd say, "You really need to be thankful you have parents (or a mom or a dad) who care so much about you." Over twenty years later, I continue to deliver this message at every parent conference, to every student I have. Sometimes, I really mean it.

Before I reveal just how horrible she was, let me tell you that my daughter has a son with autism. I have always said that God knew what he was doing when he gave Emmett to Jenipher and Scot. They are the world's most perfect parents....for him.

Tim's mother was at the opposite end of the parenting scale...she wasn't even on the scale. I have no idea what God was thinking. They say that some people are on this planet for the sole purpose of being a bad example for the rest of us: Tim's mother.

Tim had just moved back home, from a residential mental health/medical center for youth. He had serious mental health issues, being bi-polar and depressed. He was mildly mentally challenged, and he was going blind. He had about a year of limited vision left, and then he would be completely blind. With the cards stacked against him like that, the last thing he needed was a demeaning and loveless mother.

When I called her to ask about putting clean clothes on

Tim, her answer was, "He can't tell. The dummy is pretty much blind, don't you know?"

When I mentioned he seriously needed some new shoes, her answer was, "What for? All the retard does is sit on his fat ass all day." Yes, she actually used the "r" word.

When I called and asked what he might like for Christmas, her answer was, "Don't waste money on him. He ain't worth it."

She fed him, but he was starved for affection. She clothed him, but he was stripped to his bare soul by her biting words. She put roof over his head, but sent him out into the world knowing there was no shelter for him in his mother's love.

Shortly after his eighteenth birthday, his mother sent him to school with his packed suitcases.

Blessedly, for Tim, the state Department of Human Services stepped in, and he found his way to an adult living situation where he was prepared for his sightless future, given appropriate rehabilitation services and counseling, and supported by caring staff.

Let's fast forward twenty years....to today's crop of parents. Some of my students' parents are quite young. Other "parents" turn out to actually be the students' grandparents. A majority of both categories of parents are single. Almost ninety percent of them live in poverty.

The kids all have more expensive phones than mine. They have designer jeans and shoes, pricey weaves in their hair, and a sense of entitlement that makes me wonder if they are incognito children of politicians. I have heard them scream at their parents on their phones, and tell their grandparents to "shut up!" at our conferences. They use the free breakfast and lunch program, but have money to spend on cigarettes and drugs.

They pretty much all say they hate their parents.

I feel just as badly for these kids as I did for Tim. Their parents are abdicating their responsibilities and neglecting their children. Stylish possessions are no substitute for heartfelt affection and watchful parental oversight. Allowing teenagers to have unlimited privileges while having no responsibility is harmful and stunting to their normal development. With no accountability for their self-indulgent choices, I see students hurtling towards adulthood with no idea of the reality wall they are about to hit.

They are as blind as Tim and they don't even know it. Most of their parents and guardians have not given them the necessary tools to thrive, or even survive in the post-graduation world. A lot of their parents expect the schools to teach their children everything, while the same parents are too busy to be bothered with helping us. According to popular belief, that is supposed to be "our job", as educators.

No, it isn't. Tim needed his mother to step up and be a decent mother. As a teacher, I could not also be his mother. Today's students also have parents who need to step up and be real parents, not pals.

Tim's mother still is the worst one I have ever met, but there are some serious contenders out there for second prize. And their children are headed into your world.

25 SOMETIMES IT'S BETTER
NOT TO KNOW

.

Where to start? Should I tell you what a handsome, intelligent, and charming young man he was twenty years ago? Or, should I describe his photo I saw yesterday on the county jail website?

The edgy and harsh face staring at me from my laptop screen almost escaped identification, but then I glanced at the name. A former student. I see a few of them every time I log onto the site, but yesterday was different.

Having taught in "out-of-the-mainstream" classrooms for the past thirty-some years, I sometimes give in to the temptation of searching the county jail web site for former students. Invariably, I find the ones who were the most sure that all the adults in their lives were just trying to "spoil all the fun" of being a teenager. They were the kids who kept using drugs, kept drinking, kept fighting, kept stealing, and kept running away from home. Their fathers, if they were known, would threaten them. Their grandmothers would sit in my room during parent/teacher conferences and cry. Their Juvenile Court Officers would lock them up for a weekend, let them out after receiving promises of improved behavior, and then lock them up again a month later. For too many of my students, mostly boys, it simply turned out to be a rehearsal for adult prison. Truthfully, some of them really needed to be incarcerated.

This was not true for the young man on the website yesterday. He had wonderful parents. His mother was a fellow teacher in the school district; she and his father were happily married. There was an older sister who was a successful student and a cheerleader at a nearby suburban high school. However, their picture perfect family was not complete. Their son had teenage-onset schizophrenia.

When a teenager acts lazy and unmotivated, talks in a dull voice to his parents, and complains that everyone is picking on him...what's new? Those behaviors might seem normal, and they just might be one of those "difficult stages". On the other hand, those behaviors can also be early signals of one of the most serious mental disorders...schizophrenia. It's a downward spiral, headed towards the classics: frightening hallucinations, disturbing delusions, and eventually, complete disorientation.

I worked with this young man, who was helpless in the grips of this illness. He could be happy, friendly, and cooperative. Most of the time, sadly, he was forgetful, depressed, and unpredictably out of touch with reality. It was nearly impossible for him to learn anything. He was in high school, but really not educable. When he came to me, he had been in an adolescent mental health treatment center, and just recently released. His time in my classroom lasted nearly nine months, but at the end of that time, he had to be readmitted to a treatment facility. It was winter and they took away his shoes so he could not leave. He left anyway. They found him, wearing his paper slippers, before he was seriously injured.

I have seen his mother several times over the twenty years since he was in my class. Each time I inquired about him, and discovered he was being shuffled from group home to group home. His story was one of a lost soul who was experiencing serial supervised living, as he went through his young adulthood. She invariably appeared frustrated and fatigued as she told me his latest update. I saw her about two years ago at a staff in-service day, and the story continued. This time, he was having an especially difficult time with finding the right mixture of medications, and things were not going well. It appeared to be fairly certain that he was going to have to transfer to yet another facility.

After seeing his photo on the jail website, I did a quick internet search. He had been arrested several times. Once for 5th degree theft, probably shoplifting. He had been arrested for buying cigarettes for a minor. Some offenses resulted in jail time and some received fines. I saw nothing I would consider "dangerous", but I did see a "committal" hearing. All I could think was that it was probably all very frightening for him.

So, when I saw his mug shot on the county jail website, it was jarring. I remember seeing him smile sometimes in my room, with a little twinkle in his big brown eyes. There was no twinkle in the mug shot. His eyes could best be described as 'wild'. I remember his wavy black hair as stylishly long back in high school, and always impeccably combed away from his impish face. The jail photo showed straight spiked hair, cut quite short and looking a mess. He had remarkably clear skin for a teenage boy, but his jail face looked dull and blotchy. He's thirty-five years old now, and looks like he's at least ten years older.

I just checked back on the website tonight, and he's no longer on the list. That means he's out of jail, but who knows where?

With many of my other students I have written about, people ask me if I know where any of those former students are today. Do I ever see them again? Do I wonder about them? I tell them, "No, I haven't seen them again, but yes, I do wonder about them."

My new reply? "Sometimes it's better not to know." It hurts my teacher heart. It hurts my mother heart. It hurts my human heart. It just hurts.

26   SO WHAT DOES ALL THIS MEAN?

Every student is special, with a different set of skills and gifts and traumas. Every day is a new day, with a different set of challenges and rewards and surprises. Teachers should never give up on any student. It's impossible to know what the future holds for them. My job is to prepare them, as best I can, for whatever opportunities may present themselves in the future. So every day is a new pile of problems and solutions, waiting to be sorted out by students and teachers, together, in a classroom where there is never a dull moment. That is why, every day, I still cannot wait to get to school!

I truly hope some of the lessons learned from my former students are able to instruct you, also. I am so grateful for all these very special students, and for this opportunity to introduce you to them and their wisdom.

ABOUT THE AUTHOR

Teresa Holmgren is living in the house and on the land of the Iowa Century Farm where she grew up. She has taught in special education classrooms in three different states over a span of 32 years. Married, with five grown children, she loves to teach, read biographies and historical novels, write, and garden. She received her BSE in political science, economics, and sociology with a minor in special education from Drake University. She also earned her MSE in secondary behavior disorders from Drake University.

Teresa is currently working on writing two historical novels, set during The Depression. She still cannot wait to get to school in the morning!